MAKE A
DIFFERENCE
GROWTH IN
Leadership

MAKE A
DIFFERENCE
GROWTH IN
Leadership

VOLUME 3 *of the* Eagle Leadership Series for Business Professionals

Dr. Larry Little,
Melissa Hambrick Jackson, M.S.,
David Rupert

iUniverse LLC
Bloomington

MAKE A DIFFERENCE GROWTH IN LEADERSHIP VOLUME 3 OF THE EAGLE LEADERSHIP SERIES FOR BUSINESS PROFESSIONALS

iUniverse books may be ordered through booksellers or by contacting:

iUniverse
1663 Liberty Drive
Bloomington, IN 47403
www.iuniverse.com
1-800-Authors (1-800-288-4677)

Because of the dynamic nature of the Internet, any web addresses or links contained in this book may have changed since publication and may no longer be valid. The views expressed in this work are solely those of the author and do not necessarily reflect the views of the publisher, and the publisher hereby disclaims any responsibility for them.

Any people depicted in stock imagery provided by Thinkstock are models, and such images are being used for illustrative purposes only.

Certain stock imagery © Thinkstock.

ISBN: 978-1-4759-9704-0 (sc)
ISBN: 978-1-4759-9705-7 (hc)
ISBN: 978-1-4759-9706-4 (e)

Printed in the United States of America.

iUniverse rev. date: 7/16/2013

CONTENTS

Acknowledgments vii

Introduction
    You Have Impact 1

Gratitude
    Who Influenced You? 7
    Motivate by Giving Praise 16
    Appreciation in Action 25

Responsibility
    Dealing with Conflict 37
    The Heart of Accountability 46
    Cast a Vision 55

Ownership
    A Passion for the Vision 67
    All Together Now 75
    It's Our Job 83

Willingness
    The Servant Leader 93
    The Power of Humility 102
    Follow You, Follow Me 110

Tough Calls

    Who Will Step Up? 125

    Backbone or Wishbone? 133

    The Courage to Act 141

Health

    Leadership Vertigo 151

    The Heartbeat of a Leader 160

    RX for Change 169

Final Thoughts

    The Edge 179

ACKNOWLEDGMENTS

I have a gift.

This gift has served me throughout my life. It is responsible for my accomplishments and any goals that I have obtained. My gift is this: I know how to surround myself with people who are gifted. These individuals are gifted at finances, business planning, law, speaking, and leading, among others. As I surround myself with these gifted individuals, I listen, learn, and execute. Perhaps the most important attribute of any successful leader is the desire to grow in every season of his or her life. That's why we created this third book in the Eagle Leadership Series. Growth in Leadership comes only from choosing to be a lifelong learner. This is where my gift comes into play. Our team has assembled a group of ordinary leaders who live in the trenches of the everyday leadership. We asked these leaders the hard questions about their lives and leadership. These were not merely survey questions where cliché answers would suffice. We asked them to think deeply and honestly about their lives and to share with you those findings. This book is based on their answers, experience, and insight. Make no mistake; these are gifted individuals who are leading through their strengths as well as their weaknesses. The stories you are about to read are true, the examples real. The leaders come from all walks of life and from all levels of leadership. You will not find famous high-profile leaders here. There are no scripted "keys to successful leadership" or canned presentations. There are gut-level struggles, hard-fought victories, and failures. These ordinary yet extraordinary people have chosen to pull back the veil of their leadership journeys because they understand the importance of growth and giving back. This is their gift to you.

I have also used my gift of surrounding myself with brilliant people in the writing of this book. I have surrounded myself with an incredible group of men and women who have used their experience and knowledge to compile the contents of this project. Once again, my consistent and extremely competent wife, Melanie, used her gift in proofing this book. Her eye for detail is the reason this content is presented with excellence. The real professional writer of this project is David Rupert. His ability to take the vision and mission of this project and weave it into the fabric of each chapter is amazing. Some of the personal illustrations used in the book are mine and some are his. He took my notes, our huge mass of research, and wrote from his heart. In doing so, he communicated mine. Our team at Eagle Consulting did an incredible job of creating the concept and developing the structure for this book. Melissa Jackson, our COO, steered the structure of the survey in the midst of leading a growing company, while navigating the international adoption of a child with her husband. Ellie joined their family from Taiwan and brings pure joy and a touch of sweetness to our team. Elizabeth Dye and Ann Bacorn, who are more than Executive Assistants, did the yeomen's work in assembling, compiling, and organizing the incredible amount of data we received. Without their tireless effort this project could not have happened.

Enough about us. Growth in Leadership is about your journey of leading yourself and others. It is our hope that after reading this book you will find yourself motivated, educated and inspired to grow as a leader. It is our desire that you find practical value in this content. It is our passion that you would take what you gained from reading this book and choose to Make A Difference in the lives of others.

INTRODUCTION

YOU HAVE IMPACT

Whoever you are, at every level, you have a unique opportunity to impact others.

I can confidently state your sway with others without knowing a single thing about you. It doesn't matter if you're a CEO with a thousand people in your employ or a first-year intern. What you do, and how you do it, affects somebody.

When you dissect relationships you'll realize that each and every one of us has a role in shaping and molding the thoughts and actions of others.

This is called *influence*.

The college student's study habits can inspire others. The middle manager's disposition can help a company get through difficult times. A man can paint his house, motivating his neighbors to do the same.

Few actually embrace and improve on this role, choosing to believe they can live solo lives. But there's no such thing as operating in a vacuum. Your words and your deeds have consequences.

The real question is how you can advance your *influence* into *leadership?* I think it's time we lace up our shoes and enter this race together to *make a difference.*

Stepping up to the calling

One thing evident in this modern society is *we need direction*. Our world has plenty of people who attempt to lead. The problem is that too many of them struggle with character issues, a lack of passion, and misguided management techniques. From the locker room to the boardroom to the classroom—there is a lack of authentic leadership.

Have you ever been part of a team where no one will step up and take charge? Everyone looks around, hoping, praying that someone, *anyone* else will be responsible. We cling to the wall, hiding our ability. We know full well that we could be part of the solution, and instead, by our passivity, we become part of the problem.

We all have our excuses. I've used every one of them. "I'm too busy." "I don't have the right skills." "It's not the right time." "I don't have the experience." "I'm too young." "I'm too old." Frankly, life is full of too many *cant's*.

But acting small doesn't do a thing for the world. Minimizing your talents wastes the investments that others have placed in you. Playing it safe doesn't impact your workplace, your school, or your family. When you say, "I'm nothing special," you're actually questioning your God-given talents, the belief that others have in you, and the trust of those you influence.

When you don't take a leadership role you deny a certain part of your personhood. It's like revolting against your very DNA. You can dye your hair, but you're still a brunette. You can buy special colorized lenses, but your eyes are still hazel. You can sit back and play possum like everyone else, but it's killing you.

BORN TO LEAD

At some point in your life, you knew you had *the gift*.

It might have been on the schoolyard, when everyone looked to you to stand up to the bully. It might have been on a school project, when everyone else shirked and you took the lead. It might have been at work, when the boss was away, and a decision had to be made.

> "Minimizing your talents wastes the investments that others have placed in you."

You know it, and they know it. *You are a leader.*

So what will you do with that gift?

This book is meant to take your influence—your leadership gift—and hone it, refine it, and elevate it. Our society needs men and women from every diverse background to take a stand, take charge, and employ the tools to help your team succeed.

GRATITUDE

GRATITUDE

WHO INFLUENCED YOU?

We learn from many different people throughout our lives. We can see little pieces of dozens of inspirations in our character, like a patchwork quilt. Neighbors, bosses, family members and others all have influence over us—both positive and negative.

Take a look back in time and name the top influencers in your life. It might have been a parent, a coach, pastor, or a friend. As you run through the list, you'll start to realize it wasn't their fortune or fame but the simple building blocks of genuine character that impacted you most.

THIS CHAPTER'S CONTRIBUTORS

Robert Aderholt
Marcus Bendickson
Charles Borden
Terri Collins
John Knight
Frank Little
Linda Paradise
Jim Ray
Kimberly Terry

In our survey of dozens of leaders across America, we asked the question, *"Who has influenced you as a leader?"*

Not surprisingly, family members topped the list. And these leaders named others—coaches, bosses, pastors, consultants, and Sunday School teachers. The point is that no matter where you find yourself, you have an opportunity to impact, to lead, and to guide.

And within that list are some negative influences, as well. Anger, cynicism, and sarcasm can easily morph into our own character. The best thing a good leader can do is to recognize where those influences come from and eliminate them before they are passed on. We must have a lifelong quest to emulate the positive influences and root out the negative. Because as a leader, *you are an influencer.*

We also asked these 100 leaders the question, *"What did they embody?"* After a while, we began to see some patterns.

LEAD WITH YOUR LIFESTYLE FIRST

We need to set the standard in attitude, performance, and trust. The eyes of those you lead are on you, waiting and watching to see how you act – and react.

"When we understand human nature, we become better leaders," observes U.S. Congressman Robert Aderholt.

Too many leaders try to start with the program or the system and then make the people fit into it. "I admire Abraham Lincoln," said Rep. Aderholt. "He didn't lead with forced leadership, but through a spirit of kindness. His mantra was 'malice toward none and charity toward all.' He was great because of the spirt in which he led."

Kimberly Terry looks back at the effect her father had on her. "His love for others and the ability to lead by example gained him the respect of others in the workplace and their personal life."

There is something to be said for "walking the talk" in the home, at school, or in the marketplace.

"Honesty, confidence, and commitment marked his life," Kimberly said. "I wouldn't be who I am today without them." She doesn't mention his education level, his level of pay, or his titles. But she recognizes—just like you and I do—that character counts.

BE A TEACHER

Our survey revealed the tremendous role educators have in our society. We can all take a march back in time and name the individuals from decades ago who saw something in us. They invested their time and energy, uncertain of the payoff.

For me it was an English teacher who would not let me get away with a lazy adjective or a dangling preposition. For you it might have been a coach who pushed you to exceed your ability.

Don't limit teachers to the formal educational arena. Some of life's best lessons come from neighbors, grandparents, and civic leaders. Teachers come in all forms.

For Alabama State House Representative Terri Collins, it was a Bible Study group leader who, for twenty years, taught simple yet profound lessons backed up by a life of integrity.

"She was one of the most influential leaders in my life. Her values demonstrated character decisions that I myself wanted to follow," said Rep. Collins.

This group leader offered her various leadership opportunities throughout the years. "It gave me learning experiences, growth, and confidence in my ability to lead."

It's amazing that a legislative and political leader can trace her management style back to a ladies' Bible Study. But it's really not a stretch if you believe that we all are leaders of one sort or another.

"She influenced me to be the best I can be."

MOTIVATE WITH AUTHENTICITY

When you study the cultural trends of young adults, they often reveal gaps in the society as a whole. The current generation isn't motivated by power, money or rebellion. Instead the key trait they seek is *authenticity*. They are drawn to music that isn't computer-simulated, love that has no pretense, and leaders who will tell them the truth.

But it isn't just a generational issue. We all are drawn to authenticity. To find a man or woman who is exactly the same at home, work, play, and church is rare. But those are exactly the kind of people who are natural leaders. Their humble, pure demeanor is a greenhouse for growing followers.

In our survey, respondents wrote about those who led with caring attitudes. One man wrote about a family member who was "a leader who lived his leadership." When you lead with sincerity and purity, it's that much easier to implement the difficult decisions that are necessary for an organization to succeed.

No one wants to follow a fake. We all know these paths are blazed on a road to nowhere.

CONNECT WITH THE INDIVIDUAL

There's a tendency to rely on technology for leadership. We can gather, sort, and analyze data as never before with the click of a button.

The downside to this analysis is the loss of personal interaction. People by nature are highly interactive. We need others to rub shoulders with, to laugh, and to talk. "As iron sharpens iron," says the Proverb, we make each other better. Distant, impersonal interaction dulls rather than sharpens the blade.

John Knight talks about leaders who "earn the right" to lead. To watch, observe, and interrelate are the highest forms of care and concern you can give a person. An impersonal relationship is one devoid of trust. Without trust, you'll never have engagement. Trust is built over time, one small interaction at a time.

I knew a manager who oversaw more than 10,000 people at his industrial plant. It was a large, sprawling operation and he could have spent his day in meetings, evaluating spreadsheets, or hovering with other senior managers.

Instead, this wise man spent up to six hours a day walking from operation to operation, shaking hands, hearing stories about home, listening to suggestions, and sharing smiles.

He was a raging success because he gained trust through access.

SACRIFICE YOUR TIME

Here we are at the height of our progress. We have every efficient tool at our disposal. Our homes are the models of modern machines, cutting our labor dramatically. Our work lives are filled with automated functions. Every part of society is focused on expending the least amount of effort. Yet the one thing that seems to be out of our control is *time*.

It's that way with leaders, too. The margin that the modern age created has been back-filled with telecoms, meetings, and cross-functional huddles. Leaders don't talk to those they lead because "everything else" is on the front burner.

It takes a thoughtful, purposeful leader to break through that barrier.

Frank Little relayed a story about a manager he had for ten years at a government organization who always seemed to have the time to lead.

"He took the time to teach me on a level I could understand. He was an example of patience and kindness," he said. "But what impacted me most was the affirmation. I still remember his kind encouragement."

There is an association between purposeful budgeting of time with those you lead, and verification of their abilities.

E-mail is great. I use it. Text messaging, instant messaging, video conferencing and who knows what other tool is on the horizon—they're all great innovations. Technology fosters quick and easy communication, but it also promotes lazy management. Take a few minutes just to talk, and you'll see a remarkable difference.

DON'T FIXATE ON THE NEGATIVE

There's a certain style of management gaining traction that's meant to keep things out of balance. Subordinates are purposefully kept guessing about their status in order to make them agile and alert. The negatives are forcefully and often publicly stated. This style keeps people on their toes, but their toes are continually stepped on.

There has to be a better way!

Bully tactics might yield short-term results, but the long-term benefits are few. One by one, team members will fall away. There is no genuine loyalty, and the only motivation is to keep out of hot water.

If you're trying to improve a situation, what's wrong is usually obvious to all the parties. And it might take every drop of strength for you not to harp on the situation until it's fixed.

If you fixate on the positive—even if it seems mundane and simple—it builds trust. And trust is the foundation for excellence.

USE DIVERSE METHODS TO CONNECT

Linda Paradise is CEO and a Nurse Practitioner at a hospice. There, she leads a team of fifty clinical staff members. Every one of them is different, bringing unique gifts to the table of the hospice where they care for those who are at the end of life. She has been coaching to bring out the best in her diverse team.

Smart leaders assess others and place them where they can succeed. A first-year employee would flounder as the Chief Financial Officer. And most likely, the seasoned executive would do a terrible job of keeping the visitor's bathroom clean. Put people where they can thrive, and then you can build on that.

Every single person is at a different level. Every person brings distinctive talents and gifts to the table. What a simplistic, and boring, world this would be if we were all the same.

Marcus Bendickson points to someone whom he characterizes as a "boss, coworker, and friend." This remarkable description is of a man who "consistently invested in my life, even though we are very different types of people."

GIVE HONEST FEEDBACK

Charles Borden, now retired after twenty-six years in business, reflects on his first manager. "He was gentle, but firm. And I always knew he had my best interest in his actions," he said. "When I was less than fully successful, he gave me specific feedback on how to do better. I always knew how I stood with him and there was no hidden agenda."

There is a tendency to keep interaction at a superficial level. We may be quick to establish goals, share trends, and give edicts, but slow to take the time to give individual, personal feedback.

Information is no substitute for communication.

Dispensing edicts, policies, goals, or even accomplishments isn't really communication. It means sitting down with your teammate, listening, learning, and discussing. It means tightening the laces on your gym shoes together while the two of you get ready for the second half.

Some of the communication will be difficult—but it's much easier to give when the fields of trust have already been plowed and are ready for the seed.

Great leaders have to be willing to influence on all levels.

Frank Little looks back at the impact his brother made on his life. "As the youngest of ten siblings, I grew up in a home where the love was abundant, but the resources were scarce," he said. "My brother Bobby understood responsibility and hard work. He taught me many life lessons along the way."

Leadership starts at home, not in the boardroom. A man who is faithful and loving toward his wife and children can easily transfer those skills to his professional life. A woman who cares for her family has all the potential for great leadership.

> "Information is no substitute for communication."

I spend many days of my life on the road. It takes an inordinate amount of people to facilitate travel. From baggage handlers, to maids, to bathroom attendants, to greeters at the hotel, each and every one of these people is engaged in full-time service. But rarely do they get an encouraging word from the public.

How can you influence everyone, even the stranger? Find ways to reach out to everyone in his or her world. It can be a word of thanks, an expression of gratitude, or a moment to simply smile in appreciation.

Great influencers focus on future potential

It's easy to look at a person, take a snapshot of his or her life, and stick that person in a narrow career path or direction. But we can't just look at the current person and stop there. We need an eye on the future.

Jim Ray has been learning the value of investing in his own potential instead of focusing on his current abilities—or lack of ability.

"I was a wanderer when it came to using my God-given gifts," he said. "But I'm learning how to manage around my strengths."

It's those strengths that need to be fed and nurtured. And great leaders have insight and wisdom to grow their people.

GRATITUDE

MOTIVATE BY GIVING PRAISE

The road to becoming an influential leader has many elements, but there's nothing that gets as many miles as gratitude toward others.

When we surveyed our leaders' attitudes on gratitude, many were quick to point to others who first modeled the behavior. This is one characteristic that seems to spawn duplicates. Spend some time complimenting someone's efforts, and they're likely to pass it on to others around them.

As a young man, I spent a summer working at a 4-H camp. It was not glorious work, but the pay was good for a teen, it was outdoors, and there was great recreation in my off time. But the job hit rock bottom when I was assigned to clean out an old abandoned group bathroom. Years of neglect made this the most unpleasant of tasks. I'll spare you the details, but trust me, it was the worst work I have ever done.

THIS CHAPTER'S CONTRIBUTORS

Jere Adcock
Marcus Bendickson
Charles Borden
Terri Collins
Danny Garrett
John Knight
Frank Little
Sandra Locke-Godbey
Herman Marks
Linda Paradise
Kimberly Terry

But a camp facilities director made this drudgery better by simply checking on me every couple of hours. He was appreciative of my efforts and gave specific praise for individual tasks I was doing. While he was sympathetic to my plight, he didn't let me off the hook. It kept me going and made me want to do better.

His example helped me be a more appreciative person toward others.

We asked our panel, *"How does gratitude play a role in leading successfully?"* Here's how they responded.

CREATE AN ENVIRONMENT OF GRATITUDE

People adapt to the atmosphere of the organization. If an organization is petty and divisive, those who are part of it soon adopt those ways. If a group is driven to quality, then the individuals tend to ramp up their own efforts.

So it is with gratitude. When you walk into a group that already knows the meaning of this word and regularly practices it, there's something different about the people, about the product. It's like walking into a candy store. It smells sweet because it's full of goodness.

Alabama State Representative Terri Collins observes, "An environment of gratitude makes a project more enjoyable and usually leads to a better result."

Those who are appreciated show up more often, are less stressed, and are more productive. Who doesn't want that for their organization?

The polar opposite is an environment of entitlement. Expecting something because of status, or birth right, or because you are simply a member takes all the joy away from giving or receiving gratitude. Those who feel entitled will never feel properly rewarded. They'll never get "enough." So negativity will abound and neither the member nor the leader will be happy.

Find motivational gratitude

Seminars, books, tapes, and programs abound on how to motivate others. There are entire fields of professionals who devote their lives to the study of human behavior— and I'm one of them.

> "When you are able to remove your personal ambitions from your interactions with others, then you are in a position to be a great leader."

The problem is that we often find a solution and then try to replicate it in every situation. We fall into ruts and keep on driving the same road. But people are different and there's no shortcut to figuring out what makes them tick, what motivates them. You have to roll up your sleeves and get to know them. Figure that out, and motivation will come easier.

It starts with simply caring to get input, to listen.

Danny Garrett reflects on the environment created by grateful leaders.

"I have worked with autocratic leaders who didn't place much value or emphasis on gratitude. I have also worked with leaders who valued the input of others, acknowledging the contributions of others," he writes. "Gratitude is very motivating."

Some people thrive on public appreciation. To be acknowledged before one's peers is the highest of accomplishments to them. Others would prefer the thanks be private and intimate. Some are motivated by applause, others by words, and some by financial rewards. You simply have to know what makes people tick.

Maintain an attitude of appreciation

Marcus Bendickson, Chief Executive Officer of Dynetics, oversees a company of more than 1,300 employees. His imprints are all over the galaxy, as Dynetics products are used for space exploration. But he's never forgotten his roots.

"Both my wife and I come from a simple and meager upbringing in rural communities. Our dreams and goals have been surpassed and we can hardly believe the blessings we have been granted," Dr. Bendickson said. "We are so grateful. And this in turn has allowed me to focus on others, and not be concerned about myself. When you're able to remove your personal ambitions from your interactions, then you are in a position to be a great leader."

When humility takes root in your life you'll never forget that you are just a man or a woman who has been remarkably blessed by gifts, by circumstance, or by Divine blessing. When you pass the blessing on, then it changes those around you.

As Jere Adcock says, "Most of what we are is a capsule of our past experiences. Most of us did not get here on our own accord."

SHOW HUMILITY

Sometimes, power changes people. We all know leaders who gained a job title and lost all their senses. But Jere sees it another way.

"Sometimes you work for years to be put into that position," he said. "Sometimes it happens by being in the right place at the right time."

Some of you reading this can honestly say that you fell into your position. Sure you were honest and loyal and hard working. But you would have never been in your job if weren't for someone else's retirement or transfer. Or it might have been a restructuring that just worked out for you.

And the truth be told, power is fleeting. We can all be replaced. So that gracefulness

> "Gratitude will keep your head small enough to fit through the door and your heart humble enough to be genuine."

in living every day in a wide-eyed wonder of learning, of being with others, and of moving a team forward will keep your head small enough to fit through the door and your heart humble enough to be genuine.

A humble spirit translates into an infectious attitude of praise. That genuine spirit is what makes us good neighbors, living in harmony with those we lead and work with side by side.

Kimberly Terry, who teaches fourth grade, works closely with other teachers and administrators. She sees firsthand the value of gratitude for the common good. "Good leaders strive for a community, not a dictatorship."

THE DISCIPLINE OF INTENTIONAL RECOGNITION

For some, gratitude comes as second nature. But for most of us, it needs to be an intentional act.

I knew a manager who started each day with a blank piece of paper on his desk, where he would number three lines. He couldn't go home until he had recognized and thanked three people. Before this simple exercise, he found that he would become too wrapped up in the pressures of his duties to make the time. So the piece of paper would stare at him all day and remind him of the need to give appreciation.

Linda Paradise, CEO of Hospice of the Valley, has a variety of employees in her employ. And they often have thankless jobs, caring for those who are in the last days of life. So her recognition must be intentional and immediate because of the high turnover of the patients.

"I make a point to tell that person that they did a great job and made a difference in the patient's life and the family," she said. "It matters to people to hear they are appreciated."

Assuming those in your organization know they are appreciated is like the husband who presumes his wife knows of his love. "I told her the day I married her and that should be enough." This isn't a marriage book, but I can attest that this is a bad approach.

Just because you pay employees or keep them in their positions isn't gratitude—it's just part of business. Verbalize gratitude and then back it up.

GRATITUDE EMPOWERS OTHERS

If you want people to move to the next level, they first have to feel appreciated at their current level. They have to know they made a difference before they advance.

John Knight has seen this in action. "The people we lead have to know that we are grateful for them being part of a team," he said. "When they realize their value in the process, they are empowered to take pride in their positions."

We've all labored at tasks and no one told us the big plan. We're just cogs in a mindless wheel. Our work is nothing more than mindless, meaningless toil.

My son worked as a day laborer for a carpenter. He moved rock, bags of concrete, and stacks of wood. He was the one who got all the dirty work, taking away waste, loading material, and wiping dirt from his eyes for some very long shifts. He hated the work and secretly hoped he would be let go.

But everything changed when the construction company owner came by and said he needed an extra hand at another site. He called my son over, and they jumped in his plush pickup truck to go visit another home site that was much further along. It was a beautiful home along the river with multiple levels, fireplaces on either end of the house, and magnificent craftsmanship throughout.

The owner explained to my son that the home he was assigned to would be even more beautiful. He thanked him for all his hard work and gave him an extra deli sandwich.

Suddenly, the work took on new meaning. My son wasn't just moving dirt and picking up nails, he was helping build a modern-day castle.

Involving a sense of mission, through gratitude, connects us to our labors and empowers others.

HAVE CONCERN FOR OTHERS

The entire medical system is in upheaval right now. Financial pressures, regulations, and increased demands have stressed everyone from the chief administrator down to the orderly. Sandra Locke-Godbey serves as a director of pastoral care at a major hospital, so she sees the human impact of all changes in health care. It's not easy on anyone. But she recently worked for a CEO who wrote personal e-mails to each of his 1,000 employees. He regularly toured work hours and held regular listening meetings in departments.

"The gratitude he expressed encouraged the employees to do their work with pride and excellence," she writes. "He was a leader of integrity and perseverance in these difficult times."

Caring for others isn't that hard, but it's elusive. We have so many overriding worries about productivity, customer service, and profit margins that it's easy to forget the people who make it happen.

GIVE PROPER CREDIT

There are a few exceptional masterminds, wunderkinds, and geniuses who create and innovate. They rarely need anyone else. But for the rest of us who don't have that level of giftedness, we realize we are only as good as the people we are surrounded by.

And that's why true success rarely comes in "ones."

Acknowledging the lead players is important—for they are the stars of the show. But it's important to roll the rest of the credits, to tip your hat to the others who contribute.

Charles Borden leads volunteers at a nonprofit. "Constant reinforcement of their success affirms the team."

But appreciation needs to be specific. You can't get away with a general "good job" for long without having your credibility questioned. Touch on key contributions. And if you don't know the details, spend a little time asking questions and learning about the full contributions.

BREED LOYALTY

Retired Alabama State Representative Herman Marks recently spoke before a crowd of 450 at a church, expressing his gratitude for their support, love, and prayers throughout his experience in the state legislature. Surprisingly, they rose to their feet and gave him a standing ovation.

"It was a humbling and meaningful experience," he recalls. "It was a great reminder to me to continue to show gratitude."

There's something to be said about leaders who deflect glory and spread the light to those that are in support roles. It's a simple act that is noticed and internalized. Despite the tough and inglorious work at that summer camp, I went back the next year because I was loyal to that man and his mission.

MAKE YOUR GRATITUDE UNCONDITIONAL

With all this talk about giving gratitude, the truth is, it isn't always returned.

Frank Little reflects on unreciprocated gratitude. "Sometimes gratitude isn't returned or even acknowledged," he said. "It has to be given without expectations. In the end, the leader who is consistent in showing appreciation will develop loyalty with those he leads."

For me, this is difficult. When I give a gift, I might claim it's given without expectation. But deep inside, if I give my wife a birthday present, I'm secretly hoping for a return gift on my special day. It's that way with compliments, praise, and blessing. You give a good word, you expect one back.

It takes a mature leader to give gratitude to someone who doesn't know how to accept it, let alone return it.

And you know what you need to do? Keep on giving it. It's the right thing to do, and you might just break down the walls.

GRATITUDE

APPRECIATION IN ACTION

"The greatest compliment that was ever paid me was when someone asked me what I thought, and attended to my answer." - Henry David Thoreau

It's my job to study people—individually and in groups—and I know what gratitude does in both situations. I've seen it in the eyes of the greatest leaders and heard it on the hearts of those who go their whole lives yearning for just one good word.

Ask any behavior specialist and they'll tell you the same thing. Gratitude works.

And no doubt you understand its value, having seen it work in your own life. Whether you are a student, an employee, a volunteer, or a member of a household, gratitude seems to be one of those rare earth elements of great relationships.

It's one thing to study gratitude

THIS CHAPTER'S CONTRIBUTORS

Robert Aderholt
Charles Borden
Dave Briley
Paul Cheshier
Sandra Locke-Godbey
Gwen Haynes
John Knight
Frank Little
Herman Marks
Jim Ray
Kimberly Terry

at an intellectual level and another to put it into action. That's why so many people feel underappreciated. That's why motivation wanes. That's why commitment falters.

I remember Prince Charles once saying he felt his primary duty was to "encourage people." I am struck about how noble a purpose encouragement is.

We turned to our panel of leaders and asked them for examples of how they have seen *gratitude in action*.

Have a Vision of Thankfulness

In order to foster a culture of gratitude in your organization, it has to start with your own life.

Look at where you are today. Sure, you might have had some lumps and some trials along the way. Maybe you got cut from the team, flunked a class, or got fired from a job. Maybe you lost a friend or had a spouse leave. Maybe you've had *more than your fair share*.

But look in the mirror. You're still standing! As long as there is a today, then you have a chance. And that alone is enough to elicit a word of thankfulness from your lips. God has given you breath. You have a chance to lead and make a difference in people's lives.

In every leadership position I've been in, I try to remind myself of the people who would do anything to trade places with me. It's humbling, but we are in this place at this moment to make a difference.

With that attitude about my own condition, I can better instill a grateful spirit in my organization.

MAKE YOUR PRAISE GENUINE

I once worked with a crew of about 80 people. Every Tuesday, the boss would get on the loudspeaker and give the productivity numbers for the week. Of course, we had to keep working through his soliloquy. Without fail, he would always say, "Excellent job, everyone. Keep up the good work. I know you can do better."

His weekly speech was less than inspiring. It wasn't genuine, and I felt he was going through the motions to say, "Yes, I'm thanking them."

U.S. Congressman Robert Aderholt from Alabama told me that "gratitude must be on an individual basis. And the way to affirm people as individuals is to invest in them." Now, I know what you are thinking. "Who has that kind of time?" But this is one sure-fire investment you can't pass.

Paul Cheshier takes his praise to the personal level, finding good things to praise in a person's character, family, or appearance. He purposely looks for one positive thing to say to every person that comes his way.

Another way to make gratitude personal is through the written word. Herman Marks is a big proponent of writing a personal letter to those who have influenced him. "I'm grateful to have had the opportunity of working with these proven leaders. My goal in life has been to lead by example in the way these leaders have shown me the way." And he returns his thanks by sending them a note, on a piece of paper, in an envelope, with a stamp. That way the family can share in the praise as well.

DEMONSTRATION THROUGH DELEGATION

I was a young man in the military, just nineteen years old. I was serious about my duties, but when I was assigned to a gruff old Master Sergeant I began to have serious reservations about my career choice. He was tough and demanding, and for the first few months it seemed I could do nothing right. But eventually, I caught on. And even though he didn't say it clearly, I knew he was happy with my work because he didn't yell as much.

But the real change came the day he left early one Friday. He looked at me and said, "You're in charge, kid. Turn off the lights and lock the door when you are done. Don't screw up."

After he left, I twirled in my chair with giddy glee. *He trusted me.*

I thanked him the next Monday and then again on Tuesday and on Wednesday until he told me to stop, "for crying out loud."

Delegation is a transfer of your power and an indication of your trust. It's a form of gratitude that isn't easily rendered into words, but if you've ever experienced trust like this, you know it's transformative.

SAY "THANK YOU"

You might be tempted to skim this section. After all, you've been told the value of "thank you" from the time you took the animal cookie from your mother's hands.

"Thank you" is one of the most powerful expressions in the human language. It can motivate the masses and revive the discouraged. It can move mountains in your organization.

> "Thank you" is one of the most powerful expressions in the human language. It can motivate the masses and revive the discouraged. It can move mountains in your organization.

Gwen Haynes had some powerful feedback on this simple act.

She tells the story of a "hard, harsh" supervisor. "This woman seldom laughed and had a sharp tongue," Gwen said. "Most of us feared her."

Gwen had to take an unexpected afternoon off to deal with a sick relative. She anticipated her pay would be docked—as it was under supervisory discretion to grant administrative leave or to charge personal leave. To her surprise, she was paid for a full day.

"I went to her desk and told her that she didn't have to pay me," Gwen said. "I profusely thanked her."

The etched, grim look on the supervisor began to soften, and a tear came to her eye. "In all of my life," the woman said, "you are the only person who ever told me I did something good."

How many people go a lifetime just looking for a single word of praise? You and I might be the best chance these people have to feel appreciated.

As Gwen said, "I wondered what kind of a woman she could have been if someone had noticed the good she could do and thanked her for it. It made me acutely aware of the need for genuine praise for those I come in contact with. Who knows but it could be a life-changing experience?"

Gwen offered me some great advice: "We will never pass this way again—so make the most of it."

And what better way to make the most of our moments than with the words "Thank you."

HUMILITY MAKES GRATITUDE BELIEVABLE

Proud people rarely offer praise—in any form. Gratitude is far down on their list. In their minds, any kind of success is because of their keen insight and instinctual leadership ability.

Jim Ray equates humility with gratefulness. "Great leaders know they must set the tone and build a climate for others to follow." To do so doesn't take a proud, arrogant person. It takes someone who "is grounded."

A humble and wise person looks around, assesses the situation, finds the right people to step in, and then pulls off an upset.

Every college hoops fan anticipates the annual March Madness NCAA basketball tournament, where sixty-four of the nation's finest college teams play head to head. We love to watch powerhouses like Duke or Georgetown mow down opponents with their synchronized play. But every year a team comes out of Western Illinois or South Dakota State or Nevada State and topples a giant.

We love them because they are unpretentious. They worked hard, kept their heads down, and just played for the love of the game. We are drawn to the humble underdogs in life because they are real, they are genuine, and they are believable.

FOCUS ON THE POSITIVES

In a world of downsizing, reductions, and organizational change, finding positive things to say can be challenging. If you are on a losing team, it's hard to find the good since the bad is so pervasive. When your industry is on the decline, it's difficult to pull morsels of joy out of the mud pie.

But Kimberly Terry has the right balance. "Our focus should not be on what we don't have, but on all the things we have going for us," she said. "Take time to reflect on all the good things in your life. And then start finding things to share with others. "

Recognition isn't all about money—a cash award or a raise. Everyone likes a little more coin in the bank, but personal verbal recognition focusing on the positives, has real value."

"Being thankful shows strength of character," according to Dave Briley. "Strength of character shows integrity which is the base of all success in leadership."

RESPECT THE THOUGHTS OF OTHERS

How many newly promoted bosses turn the place upside-down with their bullish and boorish behavior? Lack of respect makes so many leaders ineffective.

This position of leadership you occupy is a result of someone's belief in you. You should respect that belief and respect those you lead.

If you are quarterback on a football team, you'd better listen to your nose tackle about what's happening on the line. If you are CEO, it pays to listen to the budget office about the unexpected outlays. If you are a pastor of a church, listen to your deacons.

I need to constantly check myself as I lead. Am I open to change? Am I willing to turn another direction? Sandra Locke-Godbey says, "When you are a leader, you give up the expectations you think you deserve."

SOMETIMES GRATITUDE MEANS DOING NOTHING AT ALL

Here's an interesting approach offered by Frank Little. "Sometimes I do best when I say nothing. Rather than becoming critical and damaging the relationship, I try to remain quiet unless I think it will be helpful."

If you are given to opinion—and some of us are by nature—then it's best to have one foot on the brake

It's a matter of respect. I've found that some people just need to talk themselves through a situation. Listening with a gracious spirit is the best thing to do, rather than diving in too early and shutting down innovation and self-analysis of an idea.

Be willing to use resources

The annual bonus used to be a given in many industries. Steeped in tradition, it was an expected part of the overall benefits package. But as the financial crisis and economic slump descended, those financial perks disappeared. Bonuses, financial rewards, and other monetary gifts have been whittled away to little more than a basket of fruit.

Even the basic pay rate has held steady or declined. Those who got pay raises kept the news to themselves, afraid of peer jealousy or just jinxing the process.

So, if you are a manager, you might not be in a position to give any financial compensation. Pay raises are capped and the gift bag is empty. Your generosity has to be … creative.

It might be a lunch—out of your own pocket. It might be a simple gift, a book, or a gift that takes some thought.

Daily relationships build trust

Charles Borden made a great observation. "The best way to show appreciation is in the way a leader relates to his team on a daily basis," he said. He suggests a warm smile or a personal phone call.

And the opposite is true, according to Charles. "An abusive, snarly attitude doesn't show gratitude."

No matter how much financial reward you heap on someone, if you are personally distasteful, then it simply doesn't matter. They might stick around for the paycheck, but they will never be loyal.

As John Knight reminds us, "How we act and what we say shows who we truly are."

Sociology, psychology, and good old common sense tell us people are driven by tangible goals. When these goals are met, we need to pause and give simple, instantaneous acknowledgment of accomplishment.

That daily contact shows you care.

LOOK TO THE LITTLE THINGS—
NOT JUST THE BIG THINGS

In the feedback on gratitude we receive here at the Institute, nearly every person talks about the importance of the little things.

While working on an early draft of this chapter, I was penning some thoughts late one night in an old Mexican restaurant. It was almost closing time and the staff was going from table to table, clearing the condiments and miscellaneous decorations. When the waitress came to my table, she took the small vase with three carnations off and put them on her cart. She then thought better of it and returned the flowers. "It looks like you need these," she said.

It was a simple act of kindness that made me smile. When I left, I commented to her how much I appreciated her thoughtfulness and how it made my time there more enjoyable.

She bit her trembling lip and said, "You don't know how much that means."

The waitress was the giver, but when I demonstrated my appreciation for her gift, it did something for her. She blessed me. I blessed her.

It is in the little things.

RESPONSIBILITY

RESPONSIBILITY

DEALING WITH CONFLICT

"A successful man is one who can lay a firm foundation with the bricks others have thrown at him." – David Brinkley

As a child, I wasn't responsible for much. Someone else made sure I was fed, that I was on time for school, and that I brushed my teeth. Life was easy.

After time, I began to assume more responsibility for myself. I began to keep my room, dress myself, and comb my own hair. When I didn't live up to those responsibilities, I would get a stern word from my parents.

THIS CHAPTER'S CONTRIBUTORS

Jack Fite
David King
Bill Koons
Billie Murray
Jim Ray
Lakeba Williams,
Camille Wright

As a teen, I was responsible for my own schoolwork and, eventually, a car. I had a job and a girlfriend and grades, and suddenly I was thrust into full responsibility of adulthood. And it has never let up since.

Now I'm responsible for a wife and children, a job, two cars, home maintenance, and feeding the dog. I'm responsible for "healthy checks" at my doctor, paying the power bill, and proper tire inflation.

But I've spent significant chunks of my life dodging responsibility, ducking the things I know I need to do because of selfishness, poor time management, or just plain laziness.

There comes a time when individuals realize they need to make a renewal to responsibility—and the mere fact you are reading this book tells me you are serious about this. But it won't be easy, so let's get the difficult things out of the way.

RESPONSIBILITY AND CONFLICT

It seems that every great leader has been born out of the fire. Winston Churchill was at best an unproven and uncertain leader until he was thrust into the Second World War, where his brilliance and ability led the Allied charge. Moses was just a wandering outcast with a spotty background until he was called to lead the Israelites out of Egypt. Abraham Lincoln was a perpetual political loser until he was elevated into the presidency and helped the nation heal even through Civil War.

You might think that with the right skills or training, you can avoid conflict at all costs. Maybe you think your people skills or personality will help you skip the hard times. But I have news for you. *It's coming.* The inevitability of conflict is as certain as the rising and setting of the sun.

We will have conflict because as humans, each of us is different. That diversity is the spice of life—and the source of conflict. Unless we are dealing with math, there is rarely one right answer to every problem. And even in math, there may be different ways to get to the answer.

As a leader, you have a responsibility to communicate, connect, and deal with conflict. We asked our panel of leaders for their insights and experiences in *dealing with conflict.*

BE AVAILABLE

The town of Centralia, PA, was an active coal-mining town that had 1,000 inhabitants at its peak in 1962. A fire that began in a trash dump somehow spread to an underground coal seam. Although the flames above ground were extinguished, the fire continues to smolder under the surface—and is expected to burn at least another 250 years.

The town is now uninhabitable.

Some leaders make the mistake of swooping in only when problems arise. Like firefighters on call, they see their job as putting out fires and, once the flames are out, they disappear. Yet the roots of conflict continue to smolder.

Responsibility in conflict goes beyond just managing crisis. You have to be involved, available, and connected with those you lead *before* the fires of conflict start.

Billie Murray says, "If you are connected, you are less inclined to walk away, ignore or become indifferent to things that are uncomfortable or unpleasant. People want to know you care about the day-to-day."

I imagine the town of Centralia could have used a leader who was on the ground, helping prevent the fire from starting and controlling the fire before it spread indefinitely.

IT'S A PROCESS

Emotions or feelings usually fuel our differences. We might believe our differences are based on the facts of the situation, but they are usually filtered through our hearts and not always our minds.

If you're working on conflict resolution, steering the ship back to port from the burning sea of conflict means returning to the facts. And that's hard to do when anger is seething and defense mechanisms are up.

And unfortunately, some use emotions to create conflict in order to hide the truth of the matter.

David King solves conflict by first defusing feelings. He does that by reminding people of the familial nature of their company, bringing them back to the team approach that they've used to solve problems for decades.

"I bring everyone together, without a specific agenda, just to allow the free flow of information," he said. "And a trick I use is to have everyone stand and talk. I've learned they tend to get to the point and move on when standing. "

He also engages in informal meetings, often over lunch or coffee, just to connect. "It's less threatening in these environments, and in some cases it allows for tough conversations to occur."

David has it spot on. His method moves the conflict toward speedy resolution with far less pain. So what's your process? Develop it in advance and communicate it. "This is how we solve problems."

CREATE A CULTURE OF ACCOUNTABILITY

Jim Ray is also an advocate for moving solutions along. Using the coaching methods from the Enrichment Center Group, he has created a process that works for both improvement and conflict at Children's Harbor.

It's called "Getting Better," and it's a simple process of moving forward in quality and in relationships and taking steps to get there.

"We identify deficits before they fester and create organizational problems," he said. "None of us are perfect and we will have conflicts. We can tolerate a certain level of conflict, but we cannot tolerate an absence of accountability."

For his team, everyone is expected to be "Getting Better." It's a culture of never being content with the status quo and a peer-to-peer accountability that fixes problems, often before a leader even has to intervene.

BE CLEAR ABOUT EXPECTATIONS

There is a basic rule of thumb regarding performance expectations. And it applies in marriage, with childrearing, in the workplace, and on the athletic field.

First, there must be a clear expectation. And then it must be communicated. It's amazing how many conflicts begin because the leader's expectations were held in secret. In a vacuum, the followers had to create their own expectations since there was no communicated goal, rules, or parameters for actions.

How many marriages are in trouble because of assumptions? How many businesses are floundering because no clear guidance is communicated? How many children live in uncertainty because they don't know the rules?

People *want* to follow—they just need to be led.

GET TO THE ROOTS OF THE ISSUE

If you're the responsible leader, you have to be prepared for conflict at every level of your organization.

I once had an interesting experience at a higher-end restaurant. The wait staff was impeccable—well trained with perfect timing and attention to my needs. They worked well together, helping each other with heavy trays and attending to multiple sections at once. But I sat close enough to the swinging door that entered the kitchen to know that the same harmony wasn't at work back there. I heard two men in particular arguing—often loudly, over methods and territory. A third was trying to keep the peace.

While my meal was served exquisitely, it lacked quality. The harmony in the dining room wasn't enough to make up for the conflict in the kitchen.

I'm sure the restaurant manager put all of his attention into the décor and front end of the operation, hiring only the best wait staff. But not paying attention to conflict beyond the public eye meant that the overall experience was negative.

CONSISTENCY IS ESSENTIAL

I once had someone work for me who was consistently late. It was just a couple of minutes. At first, I overlooked it. But because the rule wasn't enforced, he pushed the limits. Once a week became twice a week. And soon it was every other day.

Honestly, a couple of minutes a day didn't hurt the overall mission. He worked quickly and made up for his tardiness, but it ran contrary to the inner sense of fairness that keeps a workplace, a team, or a group on even keel.

It created an atmosphere of resentment among those who showed up to work faithfully and on time every day. It fostered conflict because of the assumptions that this person was able to name his own rules and set his own standard.

I had to step in and correct the problem. *Everyone has to play by the same rules.*

No matter how hard the workouts are on the team, you want to know that someone isn't missing out on the reps because he's the coach's son. No matter how challenging the work is, you want to know that it's challenging for everyone.

A consistent atmosphere creates a culture that is less prone to conflict.

TIMING IS EVERYTHING

Depending on your personality, you may be more inclined to let conflict run its course, to let things simmer down. Others are fixers, just ready to roll up their sleeves, change the flat tire, and push the car back down the road.

Both approaches have their place.

Billie Murray is the latter. "I like to deal with conflict head on. Lack of action or talking something to death makes me crazy," she said. But she often overlooks vital details. "By not listening, I miss out on information that could have changed the course of action."

Finding the right time to speak and act is really the mark of wisdom.

For Billie, her solution is to start the process early, but not to force it. "I like to tackle the subject initially as soon as possible so that we can start on the road to change. If you wait too long to communicate, it can only allow the problem to be more detrimental in the end."

RESOLVE WITH DIGNITY AND RESPECT

Camille Wright, who serves at a Board of Education, is often in the middle of resolving conflicts between students, teachers, and parents. One parent in particular came in. She had staked her position and just knew that she was "right."

"She was given to extreme exaggerations about the situation. But I was able to decipher from her ranting that a problem really did exist," said Camille.

> "Conflict is almost necessary for an organization to better itself. And it's the strong leader who will help channel conflict into growth."

Sometimes, you have to look past the puffed chest, the raised voice, and the extreme speech to see that there really is an issue.

"When I relayed the solution, she was stunned that I had listened and was willing to do something," Camille said.

"I've found that the best way to connect with individuals is to be honest and truthful, but in a positive manner," according to Bill Koons. "Knowing what is important to others helps me to communicate. Respect for the person is most important."

Dignity. Respect. Patience. Listening. All of these words often run contrary to the typical conflict. But they are vital to restore the individual's worth—which is really the reason the conflict began in the first place.

STAY OBJECTIVE, KEEPING AN OPEN MIND

It's tempting to walk into a situation with your mind made up, and there's usually some history that goes into your predisposition. One of the parties has probably been involved in previous conflicts, and perhaps you've even labeled him or her a troublemaker. That person really doesn't have a shot at fairness.

True leaders keep an open mind, despite the history.

Lakeba Williams believes the key is in proper preparation. "I have to decide in advance how I'll respond, regardless of the actions of the other person," she said. "'Calmness can lay great errors to rest,' said King Solomon, so I try not to throw stones or place blame. I remind myself that it's not personal."

Billie Murray will change her communication style, depending on what group of people she is trying to resolve conflict with. "I try to make them feel comfortable." It's not talking down to people and it's not talking up to people.

VALUE YOUR PEOPLE

For Jack Fite, it comes down to the Golden Rule. "I need to respect all and attempt to treat everyone the way I would want to be treated."

He often struggles to level the playing field between the classes of employees.

"It's not hard to respect the work of a fine carpenter or craftsman," he admits. "But to understand the grind of the laborer who toils in the heat of the day and to be able to encourage them is a benefit."

But if you value your organization, you'll value the people who make it work—from the bottom to the top.

Conflict is almost necessary for an organization to better itself. And it's the strong leader who will help channel conflict into growth.

RESPONSIBILITY

THE HEART OF ACCOUNTABILITY

"The world rests on principles." – Henry David Thoreau

What are you responsible for? If you are like many leaders, you'll spread your hands, look around, and say, "Everything." And it's true to a point. Responsibility does ultimately rest with those in charge. But that's not a helpful description and can even be discouraging. If you really believe you are responsible for *everything*, then you will run yourself to the ground with the details of every operation.

That's not leadership. That's insanity.

THIS CHAPTER'S CONTRIBUTORS
Thomas Baumbach
Anna Clifton
Susan Crittenden
John Dupes
Kelly Jackson
David King
Billie Murray
Jim Ray

Specific responsibilities probably fill your planner, the notepad by your phone, your calendar on your computer, and your brain at night while you're trying to sleep. Hiring. Scheduling. Meetings. Production. Customers. They all demand your time, and thus you assume those are your responsibilities. But let's pull back.

If responsibility is relegated to the narrative of a job description or bullet points in a position contract, what about the other, unwritten responsibilities like teamwork and integrity? If your responsibility is to simply meet year-end goals, then what about the lifelong goals of building excellence and character?

The specific requirements of your position are important, and I don't mean to denigrate them. But responsibility is a core value that transcends the checkmarks on any piece of paper.

We asked our contributing leaders to weigh in on *what is responsibility to them*. Here are a few of their reactions.

UNDERSTAND THE MISSION OF THE ORGANIZATION

Repeatedly, we heard that this was a vital responsibly of leaders—to understand, communicate, and implement the vision and mission of the organization.

We'll spend more time talking about casting a vision in the next chapter, but for now let's focus on the willingness to implement the basic mission.

Nearly every team, industry, and business has a mission statement. And I've even seen it in classrooms, libraries, and homes. These statements help articulate the values of that organization, boiling it down to simple, understandable language. Billie Murray advises, "Often we get too wordy and complicated in our vision and mission. The most effective is sweet and simple."

Many of these wordy statements are too complex and don't say a thing, like this: "Our vision is to employ synergy and collaborative effort to create deliverables for a modern world." Huh? That's a tough mission to implement, let alone understand. For your own leadership, don't rely just on the boilerplate language hanging in the president's office. Take time to find out what the mission of your organization really is.

Vince Lombardi gave lots of great speeches, but his most

famous one was to his players before a big championship game. "This is a football. This is a football," he said repeatedly. The point was to protect the ball, to defend the ball, and to get the ball.

David King finds two or three simple things to focus on. "They can be large, strategic goals or simple process changes to improve," he said. "Trying to do too much only inhibits the ability to move the organization forward."

"I need to understand my role and to have the correct vision myself. Then I help those in the company understand what the goals and common interests are to define who we really are as a company."

Political campaigns are often won and lost on vision. The simple images tend to elevate the understanding of a candidate. How many organizations are built on easy-to-understand goals like "Build better cars," "A television in every home," or "Simplify life"?

COMMUNICATE THE MISSION OF THE ORGANIZATION

Once you understand the mission, then the tough part is communicating it. We heard from leaders comments such as, "Communicate the plan to all stakeholders," "Tell our mission in a clear fashion," and "Talk about your goals often."

David King communicates his goals over and over again. It's not always an enjoyable task. "I sometimes feel like I'm re-plowing the same old ground, but I have found the steady reiteration of these simple things is required to make them really take hold."

The end result, according to David, is "renewed confidence in the leadership team."

Dynetics President Thomas Baumbach is responsible "to prepare the next generation of company leadership to embrace our values, sustain our purpose, and be true to our philosophy."

The French military leader Napoleon Bonaparte was known to regularly mingle with his troops at every level. He would often march up to the lowest-level soldier and ask him to explain the army's overall mission. Bonaparte felt if the foot soldier could understand it, then the mission was clear.

CREATE AND SUSTAIN A HEALTHY CULTURE

A culture of success and pride isn't built overnight. Sports dynasties are interesting studies. Their organizational structure, respect, and quality attract top talent. And the culture of quality output improves the skills of everyone who buys into the system.

The successful team is a healthy team. They like each other. They communicate. They work together toward a goal. Anna Clifton, who leads the staff and students as a principal, creates an "atmosphere where success can be attained." She does this by "providing the right resources for each team member to meet their responsibilities."

To put it simply, if a teacher needs to teach science, she needs books, and microscopes and slides and charts. If she doesn't have those resources, she'll fail.

Making sure everyone has the right tools is a key responsibility, according to Anna. "It allows individuals to continue growing in their area of expertise."

If every member is thriving individually, then corporate culture is a snap.

Thomas Baumbach sees reinforcing principles as his top responsibility. "I need to frame and promulgate a culture that dynamically learns to build companies that will last generations. We need to be a learning organization that changes to be profitable and sustaining."

The whole organizational chain
needs to know the plan

Those who write and speak and instruct must have those who will actually listen to the communication. You can have a great grasp of mission and a solid plan, but if no one's paying attention, you are just "whistling in the woodshed," as they say.

Susan Crittenden is careful to find ways to spread the discussion at all levels of her organization. "I connect the line employees with upper management. That helps those at lower levels communicate concerns to those at the upper levels. Once that road is paved with communication, then expectations are often received with an open ear."

It is a communication road, isn't it? And those of us who are responsible for a portion of the road must do regular maintenance. We have to patch the potholes and make sure the speed limits are posted and the boundary lines clearly marked. If the road ever becomes too difficult to navigate, then most will stay home, comfortable in their worlds. We have to keep it open.

The office or the desk is a refuge for the harried leader. We all face the temptation to swim in reports, analysis, and e-mail. But an overemphasis on *paperwork* and under emphasis on *peoplework* hurts your organization.

You may need to "force" communication by scheduling one-on-ones, reviewing performance, and having regular meetings with no agenda. Those you lead need your direction, your presence, and your communication.

"Vision casting for me is throwing a lure on top of the water and reeling in the input from others," said John Dupes. When the vision comes from the team, the buy-in is much easier.

For Billie Murray, a vision has to be top-to-bottom involvement.

She's seen the most success "when everyone from the receptionist to the president knows what they do is valued and part of the success of the company." And that's what you get when a vision is formed through consensus. It's not a vote or a popularity contest, but there does need to be some input.

"When everyone—and I mean everyone—doesn't know their role in the organizational vision and mission, it is a failure," said Billie.

REMOVE OBSTACLES TO SUCCESS

Once the road of communication is clear, then the responsible leader goes to work removing other barriers. Kelly Jackson says his responsibility is to "remove obstacles that would prevent my team from achieving their objectives."

Good leaders work hard to take away the distractions that keep others away from the mission. Sometimes it's paperwork, onerous requirements, new demands, or bureaucracy. Sometimes it's you—and you simply need to get out of the way!

Micromanaging has a place and a time. But once the place has changed and time elapsed, back off. For Kelly, removing obstacles leads to "cohesion and a technically-skilled team."

OPERATE WITH INTEGRITY

Jim Ray's top responsibility is to manage the operations around his core values of "courage and integrity."

"These values have allowed me to boldly confront issues without caving in to fear and inconsistency," he said. "I keep my eyes on what makes us successful."

How many titans of business have crashed in the last twenty years? Buckling under shaky structure, inconsistent reporting, and a lack of transparency, companies worth billions of dollars have crashed. When they fell, they took with them jobs, career aspirations, and stockholders' investments.

John Dupes says it's important that he works with integrity. "I hold myself to the highest moral and ethical standard. How can I expect those attributes from my team if I don't model them personally?"

Integrity doesn't always lead to obvious success. You can be an honest, truthful, and dedicated buggy-whip manufacturer and you will still not be profitable. You can be coach of a prep football team that has all the integrity in the world, but without some athleticism they will not always win games.

You may lose, but it will be with your head held high. Your character will not be impugned, nor will your values be question. "A good name is worth more than riches."

GIVE CREDIT AWAY

John Dupes looks for successes to give away, "even small ones. I give credit away whenever I can."

It's not always easy. You've worked hard, dedicating yourself to your team and to their success. But to share the limelight—or completely step away from it—is a monumental responsibility.

> "Sometimes the biggest distraction is you – and you simply need to get out of the way"

I often tell a story I heard about one of my friends in the aerospace industry. His team had just won a major award, and his boss wanted to meet with this leader to offer praise and appreciation for a job well done. Instead of attending the meeting alone, the leader asked one of his team members to attend with him.

He introduced the member to his boss and said, "Susan was a major reason we accomplished this project. Her leadership and hard work set the example for the entire team. I want you to know who was responsible for our success. "

This leader's choice to give away the credit led to improved trust and loyalty from his team members.

BE VISIBLE

There's a style of leading called "management by wandering around." And of course, there's even an acronym assigned to it—MBWA.

Hewlett-Packard first institutionalized MBWA in the 1970s, encouraging their managers to make spontaneous visits to workplaces. Some have said Abraham Lincoln first modeled it, as he would leave his presidential quarters regularly to visit the Union soldiers in their camps.

To be honest, it's probably been a mark of great leaders since the dawn of mankind. You simply cannot really understand the work unless you see it. You can't relate to those you lead unless you stand shoulder-to-shoulder with them.

The television series *Undercover Bosses* has been an interesting reality series as CEOs of major companies don hardhats and aprons and covertly perform the work of the line workers. The results—and the revelations—have been interesting.

John Dupes says "being visible within your departments is vital, every day. It shows your team that you are available. And it doesn't hurt productivity either when they expect a daily walk through.

"Most executives can easily tie themselves to a desk, strategizing, clearing mounds of paperwork,

> "Mediocrity removes the air from the room, leaving us gasping on past success and little hope for the future."

returning calls and e-mails. All of this is important, but in their proper time," John said.

So my advice? Get out and wander a little.

INVEST IN WHAT YOU HAVE BEEN ASKED TO LEAD

I was leading our team through a significant organizational change. This included a new company with a new name and transitioning from the known into a new unknown territory. The transition caused chaos and confusion. It brought upheaval to a practice that was already swamped with work.

There were risks, lots of hard work, and discomfort during this process. At the end of the route I realized that our team had chosen the loyal path because they believed in our mission to make a difference in the lives of others.

I was amazed at their support and patience, even when it was inconvenient and at times extremely difficult for them. The result of their investment is a stronger, more effective organization that is more capable to pursue our vision and thus impact the lives of others.

Mediocrity is the stuff that fuels conflict. It simply gives too much space for human weakness to grow. Settling for anything less than the best is a disservice to you, to those you lead, and to your organization. Mediocrity removes the air from the room, leaving us gasping on past success and little hope for the future.

Passion has a way of denying conflict a foothold.

Responsibility

Cast a Vision

"Leadership is the capacity to translate vision into reality." –
Warren Bennis

While there's no shortage of responsibilities for leaders, hopefully we've helped you sort out the essential from the important, the excellent from the good.

It's tough to narrow down a leader's focus. I've seen organizations that have signs on the work room that say, "Safety is our Job #1." But in the administrative area, there's another sign that says, "Efficient Service is our Job #1." Yes, when those same leaders are with their governing board, "Profits are Job #1."

Transcending all of these seemingly conflicting goals is *vision*. Vision is capturing an image of the current organization and reinterpreting for a time and place days, months, and often years down the road. Vision is peering into the future and dreaming of where you want to be.

Vision casting is difficult to do without the authority to back it up. Line workers who have a vision that isn't shared by leadership will be frustrated in the end. It starts at the top. Casting a vision is a leader's responsibility.

"The truth is people look to leaders for direction," says Lakeba Williams. "Even if they fight against it at first."

Without vision, there is rarely direction. Without direction, there are no goals. And without goals, there is no progress.

We turned to our leadership panel and asked them for their insights in *casting vision.*

Some leaders don't have the foresight and wisdom to create a vision. Some are better suited to execution of the vision rather than creating it. And that's fine, as long as it's a recognized deficiency. The best thing you can do if you aren't visionary is to surround yourself with those who are.

Many of us get too caught up in the day-to-day to take the time to cast a vision. Camille Wright admits she spent too many days "in the weeds."

"I tried to pull weed after weed, to fix things. I realized this wasn't my primary role," she admits. "My role is to stay 30,000 feet above and keep everyone's eyes on the end game. I need to show them where we need to go, and encourage and support."

Now for most of you, 30,000 feet is a little too high. For some, ten feet is enough to be able to look ahead, to peek around the corner, to show a vision of the future. So how can you do that?

HAVE A CLEAR IDENTITY OF YOURSELF
AND YOUR ORGANIZATION

It's tough to cast a vision if you're not sold on it yourself.

Jim Ray's position as the CEO of Children's Harbor is one

that must remain true to the organizations founding. "I understand what the founders wanted to accomplish when they started this twenty-two years ago. Their vision was to help families with seriously ill children. And I am sold out on that vision," he said.

A few years ago, the organization partnered with others who didn't share the same vision. "Their operational values and methods were different from ours, and we had to make hard decisions."

They severed the ties, even though it meant the funding streams would be impacted. "Every January I wake up with the understanding that we need to raise $3 million and we just dig in and get it done."

Responsibility in casting a vision helps you achieve success because it pushes away distractions.

Once you understand the vision, you will need to spread the vision. Otherwise, it's just a private dream that goes nowhere.

HAVE FLEXIBILITY IN CREATING THE VISION

Forming the vision takes lots of collaboration and patience. Dena Crow admits, "My vision may not be the best vision." It's a work in progress as you gather input from others.

It takes a strong leader to admit that he or she doesn't have all the answers. "I'm always listening to others, brainstorming together, and learning from failures," said Dena. "This is the best way to set future goals and establish the organization's mission."

If you are a leader, you have a pretty good idea of the way things ought to be. You have a goal and a plan how to get there. That's how you begin to cast the vision, building on it with the input of others and refining it. The end product may not look at all like your initial vision. And that's alright.

The key is to be flexible. Your good idea may not really be all that good. But if you are open, it may be the genesis to something great.

Hiring someone with the right skills or education is a strong leadership move. But that doesn't make them the "team."

"Until they understand the product, agree with the goals of the company, and fit into the staff, it won't be strong," said Dena. "It takes time to gel as a 'family'. It takes patience to wait for the right person to add to the staff, or you need to wait for the right person's ability to grow to meet the need."

Jane Knight admits, "I naively thought those in my network would simply follow my lead." She believed that simply because she had a vision, others would follow. "Eventually I learned that people adopt new ways of thinking in their own ways, and at their own pace."

Sometimes the vision is unrealistic. The football team might start with a vision of a perfect season, but it may need to be adjusted based on reality. The benchmark might need to change from perfection to, "We will hold our opponents to fewer than twenty points a game."

Embrace the conflict in vision casting

"My passion wasn't enough to get everyone on board," recalls Jane. It's true. You might have done everything right in casting your vision, but there will be those who disagree. I've built a career on helping people work through conflict, so I've seen it firsthand.

Sometimes those who oppose the vision have to be removed from the environment. If the group has bought into the vision, and yet they are being pulled back by one or two who are sabotaging progress, sometimes, as a leader, you have to make the tough call.

Zeke Smith, Executive Vice President of External Affairs at Alabama Power, remembers such a time.

"Early in my career, an executive saw a leader that was dysfunctional. He saw how it was affecting our team and the entire organization," he recalls. "He ultimately removed him. This taught me an invaluable lesson about the importance of protecting the team and the organization."

Sometimes it's a matter of listening to those conflicts.

When the Ford Motor Company was overhauling one of their vehicle lines, Senior Manager John Risk skipped the usual high-level meetings and went directly to the factory floor. There had been rumblings, as there are with any change.

He climbed into a car that was making its way down the assembly line. As the car-in-progress stopped at each station, he gathered input on how to build a better vehicle. His journey garnered more than 1,400 suggestions that helped the car maker redesign the model and sell thousands more.

You might not be able to jump into a car down the assembly line, but you should proactively embrace the conflict.

REPEAT THE VISION. AND THEN REPEAT IT AGAIN.

Thomas Baumbach prides himself on the vision at Dynetics, which is now more than thirty-five years old. But he's still surprised at how often he has to reiterate the vision of producing "high technology, cost-effective solutions to our customers' toughest problems."

"I'm shocked at how often I must repeat and reinforce this message."

Let's face it. Every day we are faced with a barrage of messages. From the moment you wake and open your cabinet to get your coffee, messages scream out at you—although you might not be awake enough to hear them. They continue throughout the day. Billboards, radio advertising, television, newspapers, and the Internet. Targeted marketing, pop-up ads, and cold calls all vie for our attention.

And the typical workplace has memos, stand ups, bulletin boards, an Intranet, e-mail, posters, and newsletters, each with its own load of communications.

Is there any surprise that the message doesn't always get through? Is it any wonder that things must be repeated?

We don't want to crowd the airwaves with yet another filler message. We don't want to have to compete. That's why the vision must not only be communicated, it must be lived. It must infect and affect every resolution.

ALLOW THE VISION TO DRIVE YOUR DECISION-MAKING PROCESS

Once the vision is communicated, then go to work implementing it. The vision needs to be a litmus test through which every decision is made. "Does this support our vision?" should be an ongoing tape played in a loop.

It's all part of the constant communication. You don't just talk about it and then quit talking about it. And neither should you start using it to drive decisions and then stop.

"Every decision or judgment should be measured according to these goals," said Anna Clifton. "Continuous, effective and efficient communication of the vision and mission of the organization is vital to keep all focused on the desired outcome. Otherwise, people will fall back to their own agenda."

Camille Wright, while leading a Board of Education, began preaching vision. And then she backed it up with every decision she made. She verbalized the vision and then backed it up with her actions. "At first I was a lonely preacher for the vision. Now, years later, it has taken on a life of its own."

That's what happens when someone takes responsibility for the vision. It becomes theirs. Then others adopt it as they see it effectively modeled.

CREATE BENCHMARKS SO PEOPLE CAN
SEE PROGRESS AND IMPROVEMENT

Once the vision is cast, it must be continued. The only way to do that is to show how those in your organization are performing. Benchmarks are the goals that we all need to keep motivated.

I once had a goal to lose ten pounds. But I didn't set any way-points, intermediary markers that would keep me engaged. Let's just say I quit the effort, and now I have a new twenty-pound goal.

To keep motivated, you need to see steady improvement. Otherwise, the drive and inspiration fade.

Susan Crittenden likes to work within standard operating procedures. When they are created in a framework of a vision, standard procedures provide an easy assessment of just how the goal is being achieved.

Benchmarks should be clear and communicated often.

DEVELOP A PROCESS FOR TRAINING NEW EMPLOYEES

The communication of the vision to new employees can never be done too early. In fact, it should be evident from the very moment they apply for a position. The prospective employee should know what they are getting into.

If your company is known for quality, then quality must be the thrust of the web site, in the questions on the job application, and in the communication from recruiters. If your basketball team is known for its defense, then the new player should know that is what is expected. If your volunteer organization is known for relationships and not profit, then the vision should be articulated.

Camille Wright is working towards a goal of "every new

employee has the same level of commitment as our veteran teachers."

But grabbing new employees early in the game isn't always practical or realistic. Sometimes, you come in late, after years or decades of visionless leadership, and you must reeducate. Or perhaps you have neglected the vision and now have a new commitment to involving all employees. *It isn't too late.*

Jack Fite has a unique set of employees in his construction firm. "Many of our employees are in the construction business because it's their 'default' career," he said. "Given the conditions in the outdoors and the nature of the work, it can test even the best of workers."

Their compensation is at the upper end of the industry, and that obviously helps inspire commitment. But it doesn't end at the paycheck. Jack works at instilling big-picture vision from the first day. That way, there's no misunderstanding.

> "The vision must not only be communicated, it must be lived. It must infect and affect every resolution."

LIVE THE VISION

I imagine Michelangelo's block of marble didn't look like much as they unloaded it from the cart from the quarry. In fact, many seasoned sculptors passed on the marble, because it was too difficult to work. But Michelangelo saw a masterpiece. And as he began to chip away at it, the result was pretty ugly for a while. But slowly, after time and much work, the final product, the famous *David*, appeared.

Now this statue wasn't a group project. Thank goodness. But your team is. And all eyes will be on you through the formative times. Nothing will sink leadership like a leader who doesn't practice what he preaches. Nothing makes the vision fall flat like a leader who isn't true to her passion.

Living the vision means pursuing it, even if the waters are choppy. Living the vision means following its principles even if they aren't popular. Living the vision means never taking the easy road if it leads to a different destination.

OWNERSHIP

OWNERSHIP

A PASSION FOR THE VISION

"Vision is not enough. It must be combined with venture. It isn't enough to stare up the steps. We must step up the stairs." – Vaclav Havel

As a leader, have you ever wondered why those around you don't share the same perspective? Do you ever feel you're the only one who has the burden of the way things "ought to be"?

"It's lonely at the top," you say in resignation.

It doesn't have to be that way!

A vision that isn't embraced by others can turn to a distant dream. We want our leaders to have a tribe, a clan, a group of like-minded individuals who understand the vision and make it their own.

"A vision is a great gift," Brad Schow told me. "But the ability to turn that vision into reality is a

THIS CHAPTER'S CONTRIBUTORS
Paul Bishop
Roger Boswell
Steve Cook
Dena Crow
Danny Garrett
David King
Phil Marshall
Brad Schow
Lakeba Williams
Karockas Watkins
Bobby Welch

greater gift. The ability to create a team of people who own and fulfill that vision creates a legacy that makes a difference."

We talked to our panel of leaders about *how to create ownership* and here's what we found:

- *Creating ownership involves pursuing your passion.*
- *Creating ownership involves creating a process.*
- *Creating ownership involves empowering others.*

Let's see what our fellow leaders had to say about this:

WE NEED TO LEARN OWNERSHIP OURSELVES

David King had a dream of enabling others to succeed in the race to conquer outer space. The dream was fueled by watching Neil Armstrong's giant steps on the virgin lunar soil.

"I wanted to do something that hard, to be a part of an accomplishment that was significant," he said.

That passion is what drives him even now. He's never walked on the moon himself, but through his company he helps those who aspire to space exploration. "Taking large risks and embracing the hard stuff makes it sometimes very interesting," he admits.

There is a point when we need to believe in our own vision. We need to get past the hype and the platitudes and really embrace it. Because if we don't believe in ourselves, how will we possibly get others to believe in us?

"If you're not passionate about ownership, you won't succeed," says Dena Crow. "You must have a personal interest in the goals you set."

How do you believe in yourself? How can you get past the inadequacies and really begin to trust that you can pursue your passion?

First you have to build a process that will help you succeed.

It should be built on a discipline of finances, activity, and actions that will slowly help your team climb the ladder. There has to be an adherence to the basics.

You will never believe in the plan yourself until you have a firm foundation, a solid plan, and a framework in place.

WILLING TO LEAD

It sounds funny, but some people have never bought into the vision and they've never taken ownership simply *because they've never been asked.*

"A clear vision at the top is crucial to keeping energy and passion flowing," said Brad Schow. "Inviting these good people into helping you maintain and deliver is a rewarding experience that frees you up to even greater things."

There is a certain hesitancy to lead at times. But realize, true vision should push the boundaries and defy expectations. You have to be willing to stick your neck out and chase it. But you'll never gather a tribe if you aren't willing to lead in the risk. Your horse has to be first into the battle.

A TENACITY TO STAY THE COURSE

It's easy to be discouraged. We've all been there, fired up, ready, and willing to take on the world. But as we lace up our sneakers and line up at the blocks, we look and find that we are alone.

There have been times when I've felt terribly inadequate. "What was I thinking?" Was my dream just a terribly conceived idea? Was I a fool?"

Those are hard questions. But if you've done the work outlined earlier in this book, and you are convinced that the vision is right, then you must stay the course.

"To me, passion is linked to tenacity," said Phil Marshall. "Because taking the easy road never yields the optimum results."

Great leaders have always had moments when it seemed like the world was crushing in. I remember having some difficult days at work. Nothing was going right. My boss was irritated with me. My employees were frustrated. My wife and kids were distant. Even my dog turned away when I tried to pet him.

But I would not let the vision die. And neither can you.

If you roll out a great vision and everyone buys into it, there will be some initial excitement. It's new. It's different. But unless you repeat the vision, unless you constantly stoke the coals and add new fuel, the fire will die.

Ongoing communication is important to Paul Bishop. "It needs to be consistent and constant," he said. "If I stop beating the drum, others around me lose focus. You have to continue your passion and not let circumstances dissuade you."

So keep beating the drum.

> "Is the long process in a right direction better than a quick process in the wrong direction?"

There's Power in Reliability

Ownership has a certain need for steadiness. In order for people to believe in something they don't quite see—which is really what vision casting is—they have to know *how* they are going to get there.

The leader has to map out the course, and that's generally done through *process.*

A prep basketball coach can try to instill a vision of a championship to his team. But to get there, there has to be a return to the fundamentals. Running sprints, shooting free throws, and performing passing drills all provide steps to the end goal. If he were to bring in bags of burgers, liters of pop, and video games instead of emphasizing practice, it wouldn't take long for defeat to take root.

Steve Cook is the Director of Space Technologies at Dynetics. He watched his team respond to a call to return to the moon. And he watched that same response when the U.S. Space program was defunded. They continued to follow the established steps towards success, even though the goal had changed.

"People can, and will, do great things. And they'll respond in good times and bad," he said. But they have to be shown the way.

So it is with those you lead. They will work hard if they see a map ahead of them. Strong processes, clear direction, and distinct stepping stones all help make it happen.

GIVE AWAY RESPONSIBILITY

It's easy for the holder of the vision to be responsible to a fault. It's a struggle sometimes to let go of the authority, the responsibility.

"One of my struggles has been delegating responsibilities," admitted Bobby Welch. "I fall victim to the illusion that no one will do it as good as I do. People didn't think like me, work as hard as I did, or solve problems the way I did.It was because I didn't create a process that empowered them in their job, which ultimately gives them a sense of ownership."

I once headed a large project that would affect thousands of employees. I sold the boss on the vision, and he gave me the resources and the team to implement it. They were good, capable, solid people who were cream of the crop. But to pull this off, I had to trust them. I had to give away pieces of "my baby" and trust them to treat it well.

We give our responsibility so others can achieve.

Genuinely Have a Desire for Others to Succeed

I recently met with a Chief Operation Officer of a Fortune 500 company. He had a wall full of achievements and victories, a career to be proud of. But he confessed this to me: "My greatest thrill isn't when we make a record profit. It isn't when our products are lauded and written about," he said. "My greatest thrill is when I see one of our team members succeed and grow in their area of responsibility. "

There is something to be said when others come into their own. It's like a child wobbling down the road on a bike, or an employee completing a complex calculation without help, or a forklift driver navigating a tight turn without instruction.

"My passion is to make a difference in the lives of others," said Roger Boswell. "This is carried out by empowering coaches and athletes to fulfill their pursuit of being the kind of leader that others will want to look up to."

Ownership is Tied to Trust

I remember when my son first played Little League. We had practiced in the backyard for months, throwing balls with snowflakes swirling around our heads. I taught him how to swing and how to throw. When the season started, it was a little tough to hand him off to the coach and let him play. He was my project, but suddenly, I moved to a cheerleader/support role.

I had to trust the coach.

I had to trust my son.

I had to trust the training.

Danny Garrett is known for asking, "Who owns this?" That expression is composed of half trust, half accountability. It implies trust, because Danny is letting go of his own authority. It also implies accountability, as someone will have to step into that role of ownership.

He's learned, through experience, that trust doesn't always guarantee results. "I learned that you can't trust everybody to do an excellent job. If you have empowered someone who is not able to perform, it's important that you correct this situation promptly."

Regardless of your political persuasion, you have to admire President Ronald Reagan's response to the Soviet's promise to disarm their nuclear program. "Trust, but verify." You can hand off pieces of the dream, but don't walk away from it completely.

OWNERSHIP MEANS ALLOWING PEOPLE TO FAIL

Anyone who takes a risk with a vision is bound to stumble, trip, and sometimes fail. You never know what works until you figure out what doesn't work.

"We're so accustomed to building people up and making them comfortable, that we don't let anyone fail," says Lakeba William. "Creating ownership involves creating a process of taking responsibility for your own actions. The good. The bad. And the ugly."

Just as ownership is tied to trust, so is failure. We have to trust people to do well in their own way. We also have to trust them to fail. If they are so afraid to fail, then they will always operate with one eye off the target.

DON'T OVER-PROCESS, BUT DON'T HESITATE TO MEASURE

While process gives framework to the vision, there can be too much of a good thing. I knew a manager who had a checklist for everything—from turning on the lights to cleaning the bathroom.

The standards and high expectations were well communicated. But after a while, they took the joy out of the environment. There were simply too many processes, too many measurements.

There is a balance that allows people to use the yardstick of measurement in a way that is challenging, competitive, and even fun. When you have departments or members of your team competing against the measurement on their own, you know they are close to ownership.

David King believes in process. But he also thinks there needs to be a little room for individuality. "I believe in giving people room to use judgment. Process is crucial in some things, but can create bureaucracy that stifles innovation. A lack of innovation means a lack of empowerment—and ownership. "

AT THE END OF THE DAY, ARE WE GROWING?

Ownership can lead to many wonderful things for your organization. Cohesion, profits, victories, innovation, and pride are all laudable. But the true question to ask is, "Are we growing?"

You can have stagnant sales or flat profits or a .500 season, but it really doesn't matter if your people aren't growing in trust, unity, and self-awareness.

"Passion is the womb of enthusiasm and the mother of commitment," said Karockas Watkins. "My passion is to lead people forward in life. And this has sustained my reason for existing."

This is the heart of ownership.

OWNERSHIP

ALL TOGETHER NOW

"If we dream extravagantly, we will be inspired to forge a reality beyond the straightjacket of practicalities." – Sir Ernest Hall

I played on the line for a junior-high school football team. I was a big kid and it was my job to block rushers. It wasn't glamorous, and I'm not sure I was all that good, but it was fun being part of a team. I rarely played, given my lack of experience and plodding feet.

THIS CHAPTER'S CONTRIBUTORS

Kimberly Allfrey
Kathie Barnett
Paul Bishop
Anna Clifton
David King
Rebecca Morlando
Jeanne Payne
Brad Schow
Karockas Watkins
Bobby Welch
Lakeba Williams

But there was one game when I got the nod to play for a series. The second play went bad—signals were misread and players forgot their roles. I found myself standing next to the quarterback who was clutching the ball with two players trying to drag him down.

He reached out to me and handed me the football just before he was pulled to the turf. For a second, I stood there a little dumbfounded. After all, it wasn't my job to handle the football. I wasn't nimble. I wasn't fast. *But this was my moment.*

I knew what the overall goal was, to score. But I hesitated, because I had never really been trained for this moment. One of the players looked at me standing and said this: "Run." And then he said it louder. "RUN!"

The ball was mine, and this was my moment to shine. There was little grandeur in my one moment of glory. I didn't evade hordes of defenders who fell one-by-one while I cruised into the end zone. The outcome wasn't the stuff of dreams, but I did bowl my way for a couple of yards.

As leaders we have to encourage people to believe in themselves. We need to instill such an attitude of winning, that ownership becomes second nature. So when the ball comes to them, they know what to do.

We turned to our leadership panel and asked them what they do to *encourage ownership.*

SHOW THEM THE FOREST

We've all been part of projects that just didn't make sense.

Most of us want to succeed in life. With clear goals and objectives, most people will respond. Throw in a little adversity, and we are extremely adept at adapting and pressing forward with even more enthusiasm.

That's who we are. That's what has made us great as a nation and helped sustain great companies and organizations. And that same kind of spirit is evident somewhere on your team. But it will never be sparked if you don't reveal the big picture.

We need mountains to climb and stars to reach for, but we have to see them—even if faintly. Showing people what the vision is helps inspire innovation, invention, and achievement.

Bobby Welch does this by "showing them the end result and telling them that it's their responsibility to get us there."

To tap into individual pride and energy is a huge weight off your back. *It's much better to inspire than to perspire.*

Kathie Barnett has studied the leadership ability of Dorothy, from the *Wizard of Oz.*

"I have learned the unique, effective style she possessed," said Kathie. "She encouraged her team to help them see the vision and make it their own. "

Dorothy also found ways to bring out the best in the Lion, the Scarecrow, and the Tin Man. She tapped into what they felt were inadequacies and made them their strengths. She did this by painting a picture of Oz and inspiring them to keep moving down the yellow brick road.

COMMUNICATE YOUR CORE PRINCIPLES

Many of us were raised on AM radio. The big dial on the console allowed for a distant station to be precisely tuned. When atmospheric or electrical interference caused the station's signal to fade, a small tweak to the tuner would bring it back to full volume. Incremental adjustment through the day would keep the station strong and static at bay.

Communications to those we lead may require incremental adjustments in the same manner. Some of us rely on the same tired methods or expressions to relay the message. What we say can be drowned out by a competing world of communication, and our voice is just one more clamoring for attention. The central message can be lost in a sea of static.

Rebecca Morlando spends much of her time teaching and coaching the core principles of her organization.

"It's important to get ownership off a piece of paper and into an organization's principles," she said. "Principles fundamentally govern our behavioral choices. A culture where every employee understands the core principles, makes decisions based on those principles, and demonstrates those principles in their behaviors is one with a potential for excellence."

When you give people freedom to run with the vision, they can easily be distracted. In our home we call it the "shiny object syndrome." I pick up the remote to watch a comedy, and then while scrolling the choices I'm distracted by a travel show. My wife goes to a store to buy milk and comes home with a bracelet and flip flops. We all do it. We take our eyes off the goal.

Bobby Welch gives people lots of room to roam. "I trust their decision and directives," he said. "But they must not violate our core values."

CLEARLY IDENTIFY ROLES

Not everyone will be a leader. Thank goodness! Can you imagine the world we would have if everyone wanted to be in charge? Who would follow? Who would work? So it's smart to break down projects into small management parts and have a leadership structure. If your team is big enough, you can empower leaders over the smaller components.

Some will be happy just to put their heads down and work. These kinds of people particularly need structure and order.

"Failure is almost certain when you don't allow others to be themselves," said Kimberly Allfrey. "Everyone needs to be challenged differently and individually."

"Every individual has an essential part in the process, project, or organization," said Karockas Watkins. "No one role is better than the other."

Identifying parts and then giving them importance and honor is vital.

Paul Bishop would agree. "The challenge for a leader is to

allow each member some flexibility to find their roles or niche within the team."

"It's a trial and error," he admits. And that's true. Some people may have been precast into a certain role because of their looks, personality, or experience. But it may be exactly the wrong place for them to be.

Sometimes it's a long journey to find that perfect fit. "Each person grows and develops new skills along the way. The biggest obstacle for the leader is to allow this process to take place and not short-circuit it," Paul said.

Whenever you grow impatient, ask this: *"Is the long process in a right direction better than a quick process in the wrong direction?"*

BE ENGAGED AND AVAILABLE

Encouraging ownership requires an active stance. While letting people run with the vision, don't take a passive position. You have to engage. We previously talked about Management by Walking Around, but engagement is a few steps deeper than that.

Jeanne Payne retells a story about one of her employees who had worked in a manufacturing environment. There were two shifts. One was supervised by a manager who would regularly walk the floor and engage with the line employees. "He would ask about personal things—like sicknesses and family situations."

The leader engaged in a real, meaningful fashion, and attitudes and productivity were very high.

On the other shift, there was no meaningful engagement. "The employees would sabotage the work because they didn't think management cared about them."

"I'm surprised how long it takes some to learn this simple concept of engagement," she

> "Is the long process in a right direction better than a quick process in the wrong direction?"

79

said. And the truth is, some never do. Genuine engagement breeds loyalty. When your back is turned or your attentions are pulled in another direction, others will step in and lead because they believe in you.

"Leadership revolves around your relationship with others," said Anna Clifton. "People will never really follow those they do not trust to take care of them."

Engagement should be done with the same passion and energy you had when you cast the vision. You can't be a cheerleader for the dream and a dispassionate taskmaster for the hard work that follows.

Free your people, free your time

As leaders, our time is often the biggest challenge. It's not people, budgets, stockholders, or the competition. It's time. And the magic trick to gaining more time is to empower others to do the work.

Brad Schow realizes that his work could enslave him if he's not careful. "So we nurture a culture of ownership that allows our combined talents to flourish," he said. "Plus, it opens the door to eventually freeing up my time to focus on bigger-picture things. By doing this, I keep my energy and my leadership fresh."

His insight is perfect. *You can't do it all*, and by fostering this concept in your team, it creates space for you personally to think, to plan, and to grow. You're not expected to know everything. And if you look around, you'll see others who can fill holes, who own abilities that you'll never possess.

Plan for some failure

We can make all the plans in the world, but sometimes things veer off course. To think nothing will go wrong is to delude ourselves. That's the way of life. *So plan on failure at some point.*

A huge part of ownership is to actually allow people to fail. "Don't fix things for them," says David King. "They need to make the effort; otherwise, it just enables them. If someone fails, and they tell me what happened and they take responsibility and how they are going to fix it, I'm encouraged."

Anyone who has children has had to back away and let them "learn on their own." I learned some of my most valuable life lessons from exactly this methodology.

What kind of enterprise has "planned failure"? But think about this approach. If you allow people the freedom to own the vision, planning for them *not to succeed* at times is vital. It's a healthy part of the growth process.

I'm not sure failure should be part of a vision statement, but it certainly needs to be part of a leadership mindset.

The good news is that most failures are temporary. They are the storms that roll through, break a few branches, scatter things, and then pass. We can't change catastrophe today, but we can change our reaction tomorrow.

The best leaders will find ways to rally after failure, pick up the pieces, and press on with new vigor and enthusiasm.

Be sensitive to the diversity of others

We all come from different stations in life. And everyone's opinion is based on his or her experience, education, and approach. If you are trying to get both team and individual ownership, you need to find a way to include everyone.

"We have had great success with letting people express their concerns and ideas for a particular project, which in turn made them feel they were a genuine part of the overall success," said Karockas Watkins.

Now meshing every opinion would be chaos. There would be no quality, no standards, and no direction to your organization. Can you imagine each Coca-Cola bottler being allowed to decide how to individually mix the century-old formula? Can you imagine a car manufacturer allowing every line employee to do his or her own thing while assembling a vehicle?

The smarter thing to do is to create atmosphere where each team member has a voice. You can do this through team meetings, a company Intranet, or an idea box where any person in your organization can bypass the levels and contact you directly.

There is a downside, as Karockas experienced. "Sometimes we have seen people turn completely against ownership of a project when their suggestion was not implemented." But team ownership as well as individual ownership can avoid this.

OWNERSHIP

IT'S OUR JOB

"When the pupil is ready, the teacher will appear." - Plato

Leaders who make a difference aren't born out of thin air. There's no such thing as the Big Bang Theory of Greatness. Most great teams are built by leaders who have keen insight, unmatched people skills, and the ability to make the right moves even in imperfect situations.

THIS CHAPTER'S CONTRIBUTORS
Kimberly Allfrey
Kathie Barnett
Paul Bishop
Steve Cook
Danny Garrett
David King
Rebecca Morlando
Jeanne Payne
Ian Poulton
Brad Schow
Bobby Welch

I believe you can be one of these leaders.

Translating ownership into a team environment creates a culture of success. But there's no shortcut to get there. You'll likely have to overcome some skepticism. After all, they've heard about new direction before—and it hasn't always worked. They've seen three-point plans and four-legged chairs and the five stars to success.

With all that baggage, how can you still succeed? We asked our panel *how they build teamwork.*

BELIEVE IN THE SUCCESS OF THE TEAM

When we asked Jeanne Payne how she builds teamwork, she quickly said, "Believe with all your heart that the goals can be reached. Anything less than total belief sabotages all the hard work you took to get to this point."

Regardless of how hard you try to show others your dedication to the goal, you can't fake enthusiasm. You can't pretend ownership, nor can you talk your way into passion. You have to believe it, because they'll see right through you and won't believe a word you're saying.

Your team members are looking for a reason not to believe. And they are also looking for a reason to believe. *Both reasons start with you.*

Success starts with the head but ends with the heart.

STAY CONNECTED AND ENGAGED

We talked about engagement in previous chapters. And we'll continue to talk about engagement throughout the rest of this book. It's that important. When we asked our leadership panel how they build teamwork, the recurring theme of staying connected was obvious.

The downside to disengagement is a lack of focus. Disengagement may even result in rebellion.

Ian Poulton has seen it. "Implementing a major change without getting out there and talking about it created bad feelings." On the other hand, "people expect change when leadership changes. So use that to your advantage," he advises.

Too often we come up with a clever catch phrase from the marketing people and call it "good." Steve Cook knows better. "I've seen mission posters posted on walls, but they were never reinforced. People tune out these messages."

"Solid communication and the structure behind it keep the journey moving forward," said Kimberly Allfrey. "And a touch of fun doesn't hurt either. These elements keep a strong sense of community for your environment."

> "You can't pretend ownership, nor can you talk your way into passion. You have to believe it, because they'll see right through you and won't believe a word you're saying."

BE COMMITTED TO CORE VALUES

Considerable discussion and involvement about the organization's core values can—and should—happen. There will be disagreement and debate. There might be raised voices, animated faces, and passionate speeches. These kinds of values are born out of the fire and they are tempered and strong, like steel. But once those values are established, they need to be universally embraced.

"At this point, the set of core values that the team chose to live by are non-negotiable," said Brad Schow. "This foundation manages the tension between team members. And it brings out the best in them and their work. "

Schow's healthy "tension" comment is important. Core values keep the team centered through the natural pressure of working together. There is built-in tension in just about any relationship—even the healthy ones.

Have a common goal for the team

Developing a team shouldn't be done without first developing a goal. In the previous chapters we've provided lots of ways to turn your vision into goals and promote them, but it's fair to say that too many teams simply aren't given a unifying goal.

If you're in a big multinational business, narrowing down just one goal may be hard. A single company may have a contract for heavy machinery in Dubai, maintain satellites for South Korea, and sell mouse pads to big box stores. What exactly do they do?

Rebecca Morlando directs manufacturing for 3M, a multinational, multilayered company like few others. But that doesn't stop her from developing common goals. "We spend a great deal of time defining why we exist, what principles are foundational to us, and how we create success for our customers."

Paul Bishop says, "The common goal needs to be clearly and consistently communicated and understood by the team." But he concedes, "It's a long-term investment."

Build mutual accountability

Accountability sometimes gets a bad rap. Some think it's like having a nosy boss or subordinate digging into your personal space. But accountability, when properly applied, is a great tool for success.

If you've ever been in a situation where every person's opinion is valued and equal, you know it's an amazing experience. There's no gamesmanship. There's no dodging. There is an atmosphere of discovery.

"I'm not the smartest person on every subject," admits David King. "And I don't have to be right. To challenge me is fine, as long as it's professional. The ability to stimulate each other's thinking without making it personal is key."

Accountability has a deep connection to trust. Trusting those over us and those under us creates a mutual atmosphere that just works.

"The first element to team building is for those who report to me to trust me," said Danny Garrett. "To get there, I have to be as open as I can. I must always be honest. I must be respectful of them. They need to have the freedom to be candid."

HAVE HONEST AND DIRECT CONVERSATIONS

Sink or swim, we do it together. That's the best kind of teams I've been involved in. There's camaraderie in taking on tough duties, tackling challenging assignments, or dreaming the impossible. But just a few bad eggs can spoil the dream for everyone.

A strong team is often built around positive feedback. But a strong team isn't all about handing out lollipops. Sometimes, you have to hand out pink slips.

If you've gone to the work to cast a vision, if you've done all you can to buy into and create an environment of ownership, if you've been inclusive and modeled respect, it may still not work, because of the unpredictability of the human element. It's entirely possible you've done all the right things, yet you still have that five percent who are loyal to the opposition—no matter what you promote.

It may be time to part ways with those who don't play.

"Once a decision is made, team members need to be supportive of the decision," said Danny Garrett.

It's tough to have a cohesive team when you have a lone wolf who doesn't want to join.

"We had a person on our team who said all the right things, but was unwilling to be held accountable for their time and the good of the organization," said Bobby Welch. "We called him out on it and he resigned a week later."

"We added three team members. Two blossomed and became invested in our business," said Paul Bishop. "A third wasn't invested, and we needed to part ways."

The timing of these kinds of actions is difficult, because often it takes some time for some people to get on board. How long should you wait?

Now some are early adopters while others are a little more wary of things. The latter aren't given to hyperbole or emotion. They sit back, let the emotion die down, and then see if things are going to work. These kinds of people are fine—they just need to be convinced. Once they are, they'll be loyal to the end.

The ones to worry about are those who cross their arms, say it will never work, and then do everything they can to make it sure it doesn't. And your first difficult conversation with them shouldn't be your last conversation. In other words, continual discussion of attitudes and ownership is important.

"I believe that being willing to take action on problem employees is paramount," said David King. "Putting up with incompetence is draining for a team and results in a loss of confidence toward leadership. I have left people in jobs too long—and it had a very bad effect on my team."

APPRECIATE THE UNIQUENESS OF THE TEAM MEMBERS

Unless you're working in a clone factory, building a strong team takes different styles, personalities, abilities, and perspectives.

That richness of diversity helps not only strengthen your organization, but also spawns innovation and ideas. "I want each member to bring a strong, passionate desire to speak up," said Brad Schow. "I want them to drive to what they think is best."

So many organizations fear different thoughts. Senior leadership is locked into the vision, the plan, and the methods.

Their message to the rest of the organization is, "get with the program."

That short-sighted leadership is good for the immediate but does nothing for long-term loyalty and performance.

"We have had success on our leadership team when different personalities and gifts complement each other in a common vision and direction," said Bobby Welch.

But there is something to be said for differing voices. As a leader, I want people on my team that I can count on to disagree with me. Although they can get under my skin, the people who look at the dark side of every proposal have some great value.

"Tension in a team is a good thing as long as it's founded on the core values that protect the culture," said Brad.

> "Many organizations fear different thoughts. Leadership is locked into the vision, the plan, and the methods. Their message to the rest of the organization is, 'get with the program.'"

PROMOTE THE VALUE OF THE INDIVIDUAL

If you ask Kathie Barnett how she builds a team, she will say it comes down to the worth and contribution of every person. She makes sure every person is important.

"I ensure all members of the team are valued and they know they are valued," she said. "And it starts with each of them understanding their role.

Value is intricately tied to specifics. I never understood my true value as a father until my son told me he loved how I showed him an appreciation for the outdoors. The other son thanked me for sparking an interest in reading. My wife told me she appreciated the way I modeled values to my children.

If someone would have simply said, "You're a good father," it wouldn't have been worth even a fraction of those specifics.

Sure, being specific takes effort and time. But to take a moment and encourage people tells them they are important. Ask their opinion, gather their input, and then give lots of feedback.

WILLINGNESS

Willing to Serve

The Servant Leader

"The first responsibility of a leader is to define reality. The last is to say 'thank you.' In between, the leader is a servant." – Max DePree

For years, I worked for a man who was faithful and loyal to the organization, but was an inefficient leader. He filled the position as assigned but was neither respected or impactful. After he left, I slowly began to see his legacy diminish. With time, he was largely forgotten.

There may be nothing sadder for someone who has devoted blood, sweat, and tears to an organization only to see his or her efforts counted as irrelevant in the end. Do you really want that? Do you really want to be a flash in the pan, someone who occupies an office or wears a title and then is relegated to a file in human resources?

As a leader of impact, you've

THIS CHAPTER'S CONTRIBUTORS

Gary Abney

Marcus Bendickson

Jim Boecker

Roger Boswell

Susan Crittenden

Mark and Diane Holman

Bruce Jones

Bill Koons

Robert Mayes

Charlotte Meadows

Billie Murray

Brad Schow

seen what everyone else does, and I suspect that's not good enough for you. You want to step up and set the pace. To do so, you'll have to have a shift in your thinking.

It seems that those who make a difference, who have lasting value to our world, are those that go against the paradigms. They don't quite fit the common mold.

If you want to lead with long-term impact, you'll first have to learn how to serve. I realize this goes against the grain of what you've been taught—that a leader is powerful and decisive and strong. While all of that is true, a leader must also have a servant's heart.

This is the heart of what we do at The Eagle Institute. This one principle can profoundly change workplaces, sports teams, volunteer organizations, churches, and civic groups.

In our feedback from active leaders, we heard broadly about the need for humility, service, and focus on others. "The best leaders," said Robert Mayes "are those who don't think much about themselves. They have a need to serve others. The truest measure of my impact is the lives that are changed for the good. There is a lasting importance in service and humility in leadership."

If you want to be great, you'll need to be a serving leader. *How can you have the heart of a serving leader?* Here's what our panel told us:

BE HONEST ABOUT WHO YOU ARE

Reading some resumes is an exercise in humor. "If this person were so great, then why do we still have problems on this earth?" I ask myself. With such great skills, we should have zero national debt, no cancer, and a new car in every driveway.

I know that jobs are particularly

> "The willingness to serve also means having the willingness to be authentic about who you are."

competitive these days, but I would love, for once, to read a resume that talks about weakness as much as strength. Maybe that's what followers long for too—a little bit of honesty in their leadership. The willingness to serve also means having the willingness to be authentic.

"I need to recognize that any abilities I have are gifts," said Brad Schow. "Since I didn't earn them, then I really have nothing to boast about. My job is to equip others and encourage their gifts."

It's not easy to share your failings. No one wants to be known as inadequate. But it's quite liberating not to have to be everything to everyone.

"When we believe leaders have our best interests at heart, we are much more apt to overlook their shortcomings and mistakes," observes Marcus Bendickson. "All of that builds up the influence necessary for people to willingly accept leadership in their lives."

BE WILLING TO FOLLOW AND NOT ALWAYS LEAD

You have gifts and abilities of leadership. At some point in your life, you were elevated to leadership. It's likely you are in your position not out of your sheer intelligence, your good looks, or your charm. It probably wasn't because you knew everything but because someone saw in you the ability to motivate people.

Honest, humble leaders understand their weaknesses as much as their strengths. I know enough about myself that I should stay away from numbers. After all, I'm a word guy. Once I was given a project that hinged on spreadsheets, calculations, and forecasts. I could have mumbled and bumbled my way through it. After all, I was in charge. But I didn't have it in me to have even the slightest shred of confidence in that.

So I passed it off to my coworker Kyle, who loves that stuff and was honored that I gave him the lead on the financial end of things while I focused on the marketing and promotion.

The people who do the work likely know far more about them than you ever could. Sometimes, the best leadership trait you can demonstrate is to not lead. *Just get out of the way* and let the pros do their thing.

"Many of those who sit with me have far more technical expertise than I do," said Bill Koons. "However, in recognizing and acknowledging their expertise, I've been able to leverage the individual strengths of the team to provide a powerful resource to the rest of the organization."

NEVER QUIT LEARNING

Lifelong learning is usually of the informal kind. Sure, you can attend seminars, classes, and read books. And of course, we are grateful when your first stop is the Eagle Center for Leadership. But the best learning comes from asking questions and inquiring about processes, methods, and people.

"I know I can continue to learn and improve," said Billie Murray. "I know I have weaknesses and like to surround myself with those who can complement them."

When you ask a question, what you are saying is, "I don't know." And that's one of those paradigm shifts—weakness is actually strength. When you lead from an attitude of reachability, it shows you are genuine. If you ever want to see people light up, ask them about their job at their workplace. "Show me how this thing runs?" and off they go with enthusiasm.

SET AN EXAMPLE OF HUMILITY

It's relatively easy to stand on a stage and thank all those who helped you get there. But it's hard work to actually implement humility in your everyday duties.

Mark and Diane Holman own a pizza restaurant. They have many young people in their employ who are continually amazed at the level of service the owners have. And there are plenty of opportunities to display a willing attitude.

"We never ask anything of our employees that we are not willing to do ourselves," they said. "Our employees have seen us do everything from waiting tables, to washing dishes, to cleaning toilets. As a result of this, our employees express a deeper sense of pride within our establishment, improving their attitudes toward work. Humbling ourselves to our customers and proving outstanding service to them is something our employees see us doing—and hopefully duplicate in their own service."

"Leaders who display true respect, humility, and appreciation are more likely to be successful than those who do not," said Bill Koons.

HAVE RESPECT FOR OTHERS, EVEN
THOSE WHO DISAGREE WITH YOU

There is a certain dignity that comes with every human being. They come with their own set of traits, personalities, and perspectives. You can respect people without necessarily agreeing or endorsing their every decision.

An employee who is just two years from retirement and has other plans will have an entirely different outlook than an MBA fresh out of college. You can esteem both. One has experience and wisdom, the other has enthusiasm and new ideas.

But this much is true. If you want respect, you need to give it.

There are those who will never be totally on board with your idea, your vision, or your leadership. I would be foolishly naive to give you a book that said otherwise. However, it is possible to have even your enemies respect you.

To get there, it has to start with your respect for them.

"If at all possible, I try to get along with everyone," said Bruce Jones. "But relationships can strain and I still remain cordial."

Nelson Mandela came to power in South Africa after twenty-seven years of imprisonment for anti-government activities associated with apartheid. One of the most interesting things he did was to appoint some of his enemies, those who had a hand in his imprisonment, to his inner circle.

"Keep your friends close and your enemies closer" isn't just a feel-good move on his part. It was to give them a place at the table to help make his change less revolutionary and more evolutionary.

"People can sense if a leader is self-serving in their questions, behaviors, and decision making," said Jim Boecker. "People respect, respond, and rally behind leaders who don't exhibit behaviors rooted in personal interests or perceived hidden agendas."

BE WILLING TO LISTEN TO THE TEAM

Have you ever "zoned out"? I've done it watching a basketball game. I've done it while driving. And I've done it while others have been telling me their opinions. The disrespect to them is wrong and certainly stifles their willingness to serve.

Sometimes I listen but am not really open to any other direction. By my inaction I shut people down. The problem is when I've gone to all this work to aspire others to high standards and excellence, my disinterest shuts down any innovation or participation.

"Rather than leverage my authority or even that of the organization, I call the team to excellence," said Gary Abney. "They work for higher purposes, and I don't want my own preferences to get in the way."

It's easy to get locked into a certain direction, focusing on the goal and unwilling to listen to anything that could possibly distract you. The CEO of a large aerospace engineering company told me that his office door is literally always open, unless he's in a meeting. He encourages employees to "drop in" to say hi or to even go to lunch with him.

He sets boundaries. The drop-in time isn't meant to undermine the authority of his leaders. He frequently walks around campus and speaks to the team, learning about the culture they live in. He's available to listen—and that opens doors.

SHARE THE WEALTH

No one likes to see the coach get all the glory for a victory when the players are the ones with the bruises, the strained muscles, and the tired bones. But it happens, doesn't it? We are in a society that elevates the leadership—the superstar—and forgets about the rest of the players.

Serving others means you are quick to spread accolades to those around you. And it also means you are dispensing praise when you see something good on a daily basis. "Give credit when credit is due," advises Susan Crittenden. "By doing so, it helps those we lead to be more willing to assist. They like working with humble leaders."

I've seen many people give credit away in almost a haphazard way. They thank the team, thank the workers, and thank the providers and suppliers in almost a rote fashion. It's almost as if they know they need to share credit, but it isn't from the heart.

A good way to do that is to be specific. To continue the football analogy, I watched a quarterback once avoid the cliché "thanks to the line, thanks to the defense, thanks to the fans." Instead, he named specific instances. "Williams threw a block that opened up the hole for us to get that big running play. And Sanders gave a head fake that allowed me to throw to his right for an open completion. And the coach called that running play on third down that was brilliant."

He missed some players and plays—and that's okay. Even if you don't name everyone specifically, it still shows you are paying attention.

"When things don't go so well, take responsibility," advises Marcus Bendickson. "When things are going great, give the team credit."

The wake of influence

"People need to know you really care," Roger Boswell told us. And he's right. If you don't care about the mission, the vision, or the individuals that surround you, you'll never be successful.

"People don't need a talking head. They need to know you have their best interest in mind. I have found that the best responses come when I just go in and serve," Roger said.

Influencing people to do their jobs is much better than telling them to do their jobs. Influencing players to perform gets better results than yelling at them to do so. Influencing children to higher expectations is much more effective than nagging them.

"This kind of impact grows exponentially," said Brad Schow. "They take on the mantle of leadership and soon they become leaders—and influencers."

Brad describes this growing impact as a "Wake of Influence."

HAVE OTHERS INTERESTS ABOVE YOUR OWN

When I get up in the morning, the first face I see is mine. And usually, the last face I see is mine. From the dawning to the closing of day it's usually all about me. My needs, my desires, my plans are all part of a primordial urge to survive.

So it takes a conscious effort to elevate the needs of others before yours.

"True leaders need to put their own personal needs or agendas aside and work for what is best for the group as a whole," said Charlotte Meadows.

Putting others' interests has a funny way of meeting your own interests. Again, it's another paradigm shift. If you want your needs met, see to it that others get theirs fulfilled.

If you are a leader because of a personal agenda to get ahead, to gain more power or wealth, you'll be exposed. "If the service isn't done with humility, people will realize your real motives and the influence will not be positive," reminds Marcus Bendickson.

Andrew Smith ties this chapter up with his poignant summary: "Humility is essential as we're all just people, full of emotion, and every one of us is capable of both success and failure."

WILLING TO SERVE

THE POWER OF HUMILITY

"Everybody can be great, because anybody can serve." – *Martin Luther King.*

"We plant seeds that will flower as results in our lives, so best to remove the weeds." —*Dorothy Day*

Being willing to serve others resonates at a deep level. Instinctively we know it's how we should we act. Whether you've been influenced by family members, religious teaching, or positive role models, you know the value of service from a human perspective.

"Service implies respect given to others," said Ian Poulton. "The better leaders are the ones who give and share and expect nothing in return."

It does fly in the face of modern thinking. Many of these concepts won't reconcile with what you

THIS CHAPTER'S CONTRIBUTORS
Robert Aderholt
Marcus Bendickson
Jim Boecker
Susan Crittenden
Jack Fite
Bruce Jones
Robert Mayes
Billie Murray
Ian Poulton
Brad Schow

are hearing in the media, in pop culture, and from those in your circle. *But you know it's true.*

Being willing to serve isn't just an esoteric feel-good concept. It can actually impact the bottom line. It can change an entire organization, creating efficiency and prosperity.

We asked our panel, *what does a positive attitude toward service look like?* Their answers give us great insight.

BUILDING A BRIDGE

I see far too many chasms in organizations. I stand at the edge and look down—and it's a terribly steep fall with no bottom. And standing on one side of that chasm, sometimes I can almost reach out and touch the other. *The two sides are that close.* In other situations, the divide is expansive.

But I believe in bridging the divide, no matter how great. I've seen it done in the worst and the best of situations, and it can be fixed in your world.

The Niagara Falls suspension bridge was an idea born in the fertile mind of William Merritt in 1846. He wanted a way to span the chasm that separated Canada and the United States, opening doors for both commerce and culture.

Most experts agreed it couldn't be done. The span was too great. But Merritt still dreamed.

One day, while watching children fly their kites over the falls, he came up with an idea. He sponsored a contest and paid $5 to the first one who could loft their kite to the other side. Sure enough, one lad did it, and the kite string was secured with a strong stake.

Meticulously, Merritt strung a larger cord across the divide, using the kite string as a guide. Then he pulled a heavier line, then a rope, and finally a wire cable. From this beginning a bridge was built.

Sometimes, building a bridge seems impossible. Critics on both sides will tell you it cannot be done. But if you can float a string of service to each other—across the chasm—it may one day lead to a bridge.

It starts with just being authentic.

"When I see leaders extend their sphere of caring and service to other groups in need, I find that a bridge of trust and influence is established," said Marcus Bendickson. "And it's strong enough to weather some very tough storms."

A POSITIVE ATTITUDE LEADS TO A BETTER WORK FLOW

Efficiency in anything, whether it's a volunteer organization that delivers meals to seniors or a Fortune 500 company producing products or a country church ministering to the faithful, is to be commended. We should all be looking for the best way to do business.

But the efficiency of service is interrupted when negative attitudes move in. At this point the organizational plan takes a back seat to individual agendas, and that's never good.

"A positive attitude helps the work flow easier and more efficiently," observes Susan Crittenden. When everyone has an attitude of service, then egos, territories, and pride leave the room.

Congressman Robert Aderholt told me to "Take the time to affirm people as individuals."

ALLOWS OTHERS TO ACCEPT THEIR SUCCESS—AND FAILURES—FREELY

Having a willing attitude of service is liberating to the team. We all need space to be free to succeed—and to fail. And having an atmosphere where we all respect each other enough to serve gives enough margins for both of these extremes.

"When each member of our team has an attitude of service, it frees up our ability to perform," said Brad Schow. "We have the freedom, knowing each of those around us is ready and willing to do what it takes if one member is struggling."

Think about it. If you can go full out, knowing that someone has your back, would you act any differently? Would you take more risks if you knew that a fellow team member would be willing to step up if you fail?

Brad has seen the downside of not serving each other. "It frustrates progress because people are more concerned with the importance of what they are doing than with the team. It greatly hinders our organization."

Jeffrey Immelt, CEO of General Electric, has seen his share of success and failure. But the possibility of either doesn't frighten him. "Surviving a failure gives you confidence. Failures are great learning tools," he said. And what better way to use them than as a springboard, if they happen to you in a community that is willing to come up behind, prop you up, and launch you to success.

DESTROY FEAR

Today's world is full of fear. Our current political system thrives on scaring people. Fear of enemies. Fear of cultures. Fear of the future. Fear of the other side.

And the economy hasn't helped, as we all fear our future stability. Will we have enough money? Is there any place that is secure?

> "Fear is at the root of the law of diminishing returns. The more energy you expend using fear, the fewer positive results you'll achieve."

Given the current economic uncertainty and social instability, fear impacts many families.

Many of those you lead and serve come into your organization with some built-in fear. They may have had previous leaders who believed in motivating by fear.

Roman Emperor Caligula ruled with an iron fist. His singular management tool was summed up in his statement: "Let them hate me, so long as they fear me." He got results, but eventually his own bodyguards turned on him.

"Too many company cultures operate with a basis of fear," said Ian Poulton. "That creates a subculture of people who are just looking out for themselves. It's just a service to self."

The autocrat elevates fear to such a place of prominence that it degrades performance. Fear causes team members to retreat to individualism because they are concerned about mere survival.

Fear is at the root of the law of diminishing returns. The more energy you expend using fear, the fewer positive results you'll achieve.

Have an appreciation for diversity

Those that have an attitude of service embrace the rich diversity of who we are as people.

Take a look around you at your team. There are Lions, Camels, Turtles, and Monkeys—different personalities and abilities. People have come into your circle from one of any of a thousand different walks of life. Some leaders try to make everyone toe the same line; perform the same way, with exactly the same output. That approach never works.

Standardization has been a buzzword in the corporate world. It strives to simplify process. That's why the counter line at every McDonald's looks the same. That's why every clerk at the grocery store asks the same questions. The process is part of corporate success. But within standardization, you are dealing with people who are very different.

You have to figure out how all those different personalities come together, like a big puzzle, to form a picture.

"As a leader, it's our responsibly to take the time to learn and understand those different personalities," said Bruce Jones. "You don't want to put someone with a bad attitude over your marketing," he advises. "Put them in the best position for them to succeed."

Don't regard differences as a threat. Just because someone has a different approach doesn't mean they are against you. The smart leader will find a way to use that diversity to their benefit. I've found within every criticism is a hint of truth.

When you invite everyone to the table with open arms, you'll find the diversity refreshing. The more diverse your team, the more options you have.

A POSITIVE ATTITUDE STARTS INTERNALLY AND SPILLS OUT EXTERNALLY

I have to make an admission here. I've gone to presentations where I'm expected to be an optimistic, forward-looking influence. I present ideals and models for success that often rely on a positive attitude. But I haven't always been internally positive. I might have had words with my wife, or am concerned about one of my children, or perhaps am in disagreement with a coworker.

It happens to all of us. We have internal strife, yet externally we still have to perform. We can do this for a little while, but eventually the seams split open. We can power our way through using grit and determination, but if negativity is the rule of order, the power will diminish.

Your organization's mission might be to serve the customer in a friendly, customer-first manner, and that is your top priority.

But let me challenge this. Instead, your first priority should be treating *each other* with a positive attitude of service. Far too often we focus on our external appearance without first cleaning our house inside.

"The more a team practices an attitude of service among themselves, the easier it is for them to serve others outside the team," Robert Mayes says.

A company that is rife with internal divisions has a hard time turning out a good product. A team that is fighting in the locker room rarely comes together on the playing field. A volunteer group that doesn't serve each other first will have a hard time serving others.

CREATE A FAMILY ENVIRONMENT

Not everyone comes from a stable, loving home. But we at least can relate to what this should look like. It's a place where people laugh and learn while they work together at life. It's a place where success is celebrated and failure jointly shared. It's a place that breeds success because it's all performed in an environment of respect and concern.

Translating the family environment into your organization takes work. Sometimes, it takes several generations of participants to develop that attitude. But it can be done.

Jim Boecker was able to implement a family atmosphere in a difficult work environment, but it took some deliberate actions. His employer acquired an idle factory and hired back some of the previous operators. Of course, the workers presumed more of the same of what they left--distant, disengaged management. They got something far different.

> "A volunteer group that doesn't serve each other first will have a hard time serving others."

"We went out of our way to communicate and engage the employees in our business plans," Jim recalls. "We gave them a sense of security." They worked side by side with employees to launch the factory and start putting out product.

"They couldn't believe managers at our level were so engaged, because it was the exact oppose to the previous companies' culture. After time, it really was a family environment."

Who wouldn't want to be involved in a place like this, as either a leader or a follower? "We all served each other as we strived towards a common goal," said Jim.

Willingness to serve each other in your organization spills out into the world, too. If you are serving each other, you'll serve your customers. And you'll be known as an organization that serves the community.

"You can tell the difference," said Billie Murray. "Those who are self-serving are really not engulfed by the team." They're not part of the family.

TEAR DOWN WALLS

When you begin to serve each other in the everyday, then when big events occur, it's natural to do the extraordinary.

Jack Fite had an employee with a life-threatening disease. "We all pitched in and raised money to help him. By getting the employees involved, they had ownership in the satisfaction of serving that person and giving back."

The opportunities to serve will then expand to the community.

"We now have a charitable contribution committee that reviews and evaluates the many requests we receive," said Jack. "We encourage them to allow the company to be involved in the things that are important to them."

WILLING TO SERVE

FOLLOW YOU, FOLLOW ME

"You cannot be a leader, and ask other people to follow you, unless you know how to follow, too." – Sam Rayburn

THIS CHAPTER'S CONTRIBUTORS

Gary Abney

Martin Bendickson

Jim Boecker

Donna Brewington

Susan Crittenden

Jack Fite

Diane Holman

Bruce Jones

Bill Koons

Robert Mayes

Billie Murray

Jim Parrish

Ian Poulton

Andrew Smith

Brad Schow

A service-oriented leader is like a faithful truck on a farm. There might be a little bit of rust on the floorboards, and it might throw a little smoke. It's not flashy. It's never flamboyant.

But on a cold autumn morning, when the entire operation of the ranch needs a dependable piece of machinery, it starts. *It just works.*

Service-oriented leaders may not grace the cover of *Inc.* or *Fast Company*. They won't guest host on CNBC. They won't win any awards for style.

But when they are in charge,

things get done. There's no hill too steep, no ditch too deep, no job too tough.

They influence through a surreptitious style. It's by the steady course of doing the hard work that the field gets plowed.

This stealth service is the kind of leadership that never puts into question morals or ethics, it never violates the sense of right or wrong, and it's firm but fair in all things.

"If you look at the language of service-oriented leaders, you will hear 'we' a lot," observes Jim Parrish. "It's the simplest of comments that reflect the heart of a leader and shows where their true passion is."

This kind of communication—this kind of leadership—creates followers.

If you don't serve, others won't want to serve you—or their peers or customers. *What are some other traits of a service-oriented leader?* And what are the opposite characteristics of such a leader? We asked our panel for their feedback.

CREATES LOYALTY VERSUS JEALOUSLY AND INSECURITY

I'm aware of the importance of winning and losing," said Bruce Jones. "And losing is never fun."

But it is possible to lose and still have some dignity. "If a player knows a coach is concerned about them as an individual, then they will give their all because they don't want to let you down," he said.

This is loyalty, and it's something lacking on many fronts today.

Employees are no longer loyal to their team, to their employer, or to their organization. Just ask a typical thirty-year-old educated worker and they'll tell you: if a better deal comes along, they'll take it. It's hard to get buy-in and commitment if an employee is always scouring the help-wanted ads.

But who can blame them? The culture in America has shifted away from employers who cared for their employees. There was a time when employee housing wasn't too much to ask in some situations. Benefits, health care, stock options, and generous personal time were the norm. Now, with continued reductions, they are the exception.

> "Care about your people and they return the favor with loyalty."

And along with the security of benefits, the security of employment is gone. It's nothing for an employer to lay off a few thousand here and there to maintain the bottom line, to keep the stock price elevated. Every number represents a family in turmoil, an individual whose self-worth is suddenly in question, and a company losing valued experience.

No wonder American companies don't have dedication from their workers, as benefits decline and off-shore outsourcing looms.

But it's not too late to create loyalty at the personal level. You probably aren't in a position to make decisions regarding overall employment, but you can do your part. Care about your people and they return the favor with loyalty.

DISPLAYS PASSION VERSUS APATHY

Several years ago at a prominent U.S. zoo, a polar bear's habitat underwent a major remodel. For months, the large beast was kept in a small cage where he paced incessantly. His lonely stare out the bars of the cells caught more than one child's pity. When the habitat was finished, it was a work of art, replete with floating logs and deep pools and everything a captive bear could want.

The big moment had come. The bear's door flung open, and he boldly stalked out into his new world. He gazed at the scene, taking in the elaborately staged environment. He sniffed the air, turned around, and went back to his cage to sleep. He had forgotten how to live and chose to be miserably trapped. Far too many of us feel trapped in the cages of our responsibility. We want an out. We need relief. But the keys are hanging, the door is swinging free, and yet we never flee the bondage. We remain shackled to our desks, to our backhoes, to our delivery vehicles. Day after day, year after year we "endure."

It doesn't have to be this way. The answer is found in passion, and for leadership it's infectious.

If you're simply rolling back to the den, then those around you will be uninspired. If you don't care about quality or winning or growth, then neither will they.

"A service-oriented leader has a passion that isn't self-serving," said Jim Boecker. "They establish credibility by actions and create an environment where people want to be accountable and responsible."

Who wants to live in a zoo, where everyone is content with his or her place and no one ever knows freedom?

GAINS RESPECT FROM OTHERS
VERSUS ALIENATING OTHERS

I worked at a restaurant as a teenager. The boss had been particularly rough on me, telling me in front of the waitresses I was trying to impress that I wasn't cleaning the seats in the booths. He was probably right. But he insulted me. He embarrassed me.

He tried to get me to respect him by showing me he was the boss. At every step of the way I felt alienated and embarrassed. Unfortunately, there was no buffer and, as a kid, I felt powerless.

I have to admit I was very good at being a bad teenager. So I got back at him. On my way out of the locker room, I snatched a brand new bottle of ketchup and stuck it in my coat pocket. That's right, a bottle of Heinz ketchup. Obviously, all logic had departed my young mind. I felt totally justified and vindicated. "That'll teach him!" I thought.

No doubt, the boss was badly shaken when the ketchup inventory didn't match up that night.

To compound things, I couldn't just throw the ketchup away. I was too thrifty for that. I put the bottle of ketchup in the refrigerator at home and then had to explain to my astute mother how it just "showed up."

You probably have your own description of employees like me. But we'll save that for another book. What kind of leadership makes followers do such imprudent things?

Andrew Smith calls leaders like this man at the restaurant "intolerant and impatient."

As leaders, we can do much to inspire great things. On the other hand, we can feed foolishness through alienation, fear, and intimidation.

"Those who aren't service-oriented tend to use power and authority," said Marcus Bendickson. "People who work under them do their jobs, but begrudgingly and without the joy and sense of pride associated with a servant leader."

> "The attitude of the whole reflects the leadership of one"

WILLING TO DO WHATEVER IT TAKES
VERSUS BLAMING OTHERS

"A service-oriented leader is willing to do whatever it takes to complete the job," according to Susan Crittenden. "People tend to respect leaders who walk the talk and are willing to do whatever they ask others to do."

Selfishness is one of the darker sides of poor management. These kinds of people never walk the talk, and whenever things go wrong—an operation crumbles, a schedule is delayed, a team loses—they are the first to blame others.

"Regardless of your personal strengths, the leader who is all about himself will use all sorts of techniques to motivate his team," said Gary Abney. "But none of them will be built on respect."

If your team doesn't respect you but simply follows orders out of fear or trained compliance, then your results will be short-lived. "These kinds of people use their skills in order to use people," Gary said.

However, if you don't blame others and you roll up your sleeves, you will see others begin to march in your steps.

"The attitude of the whole reflects the leadership of one," said Susan.

Builds solid relationships versus leading by dictatorship

There's a time for barking orders. When it comes to safety, or immediacy, or urgency, there's just not the time for explanation. My father rarely spoke loudly and hardly ever raised his voice. But when he did, it got my attention.

And those you lead should understand the situation because these kinds of requests are infrequent.

For example, consider the battlefield. Military training is arduous, vigorous, and methodical. It's not done without lots of prep work. It's meant to institute tremendous trust in leadership to make the right decisions when necessary.

The mission is performed through building relationships—one moment at a time.

"A service-oriented leader understands the value of building relationships and encouraging others to do the same," said Robert Mayes. "On the other hand, a leader who isn't oriented toward serving others consumes relationships."

Puts people first versus being
driven solely by profits

Some leaders are consumers of people. They use those they lead as commodities, things to satisfy a hunger, to reach a goal.

"They view an employee's worth only as it relates to their contribution to the corporate bottom line," said Robert. "A servant leader appreciates the necessity of profits, but within the context of caring for those who choose to be part of the organization."

"On the other hand, a leader who doesn't understand service is only interested in how their followers can help meet the goals," said Robert.

As harsh as this seems, we've all done it. We've mentally sorted those we lead by the contributors and the non-contributors. Those who are on the bottom are the "vital few" that need the most attention. The one-time CEO of General Electric, Jack Welch, famously preached the concept of promoting the top 10 percent of the workforce and firing the bottom 10 percent each year.

There is a necessity to run your organization efficiently, and the best way to evaluate that is to assign number values to those under your leadership. But here are two truths:

- People aren't numbers.
- Numbers don't always tell the whole story.

"A service-oriented leader should be a person who is known for the way they treat others—people, employees, customers," said Diane Holman. "They should show the highest respect."

COMMUNICATES WITH CLARITY AND
CONSISTENCY VERSUS ISOLATING OTHERS

Some people do well in isolation. They work alone and they are happy. Thank goodness for people who can man toll booths, write computer code into the dark night, and clean office buildings after hours.

"Just leave me alone." They don't want to hear from the boss, and they don't offer anything up beyond the minimum. While these kinds of people are necessary, they are generally a rare breed. Most of us need communication, because within the bookends of a conversation—either verbal or written—are the necessities for motivation, encouragement, and human worth.

"They need to clearly define what others are to do and then equip them well," said Brad Schow.

We can manipulate others through our silence. They will pine away in obscurity never knowing if they are necessary, valued, or even noticed.

The satirical comedy *Office Space* shines a light on the terrible supervisor, Bill Lumbergh. One of the saddest characters in the movie is Milton, who has been moved to the basement and even had his favorite red stapler confiscated. Every conversation from Milton is cut off, every question dismissed, every thought squashed. Even his paycheck is mysteriously delayed for weeks. He is marginalized by isolation.

No one really wants to work that way. In your organization, isolation is a death knell. If you have those who prefer to work independently, you still are obligated to communicate goals, progress, and expectations. They may outwardly resent it, but deep down inside they appreciate your effort.

PURSUES EXCELLENCE VERSUS PERSONAL RECOGNITION

We heard from a female leader whose boss had her fill out his yearly reviews with *her* accomplishments. "Tell me all the things you've done this year." He would then copy and paste those accomplishments into his evaluation.

That's a great way to reduce innovation, creativity, and endeavors.

The service-oriented leader does the right thing without expecting something in return," Marcus Bendickson said. "He invests in others because he cares for them and considers them valuable. He never keeps track of who owes who."

You can always tell a leader who is pursing goals for his or her own recognition versus someone who is genuinely pursing excellence.

Billie Murray takes this a step further. She thinks a lack of investment in future leaders is a sure sign of a leader who doesn't embrace service. "They promote self-centered behavior and never have a succession plan."

On the other hand, a healthy leader is never threated by promising upstarts.

"They develop others with no fear of job protection," said Ian Poulton.

"When a leader builds an organization framed in the context of pursuing excellence, they value people for who they are," said Robert Mayes.

ENTRUSTS OTHERS WITH RESPONSIBILITY
VERSUS MICROMANAGING

The effective leader will balance personal involvement with corporate ownership. Leading and participating at all levels demonstrates the essence of teamwork. Micromanaging demonstrates a lack of trust and respect for the team.

"A strong leader motivates through doing and participating at all levels," observes Ian.

An effective leader must lead by example and be willing to do whatever it takes to accomplish the goal. Participation in the process doesn't mean micromanaging. Conversely, it means holding those you lead accountable.

At Eagle Consulting, we have developed accountability metrics that allow our team to take responsibility for their clients, yet submit to an ongoing reporting process. This allows our leaders to interact weekly with their team while not micromanaging their coaching sessions.

Strong team members view accountability as promoting growth opportunities. They become frustrated with feeling micromanaged, sensing a lack of belief in their ability to be successful.

Nothing kills a motivated team more quickly than micromanagement. "Don't manage every aspect of their endeavors," Bobby Welch said. "If you don't trust the little things, they will never embrace the level of ownership that you desire them to have. While I don't micromanage, I do hold them accountable."

FOSTERS TEAM GROWTH VERSUS ALLOWING TEAM DYSFUNCTION

Ian Poulton also observes that unhealthy leaders alienate followers from each other, from their peers, and from leaders.

"They just lose respect," he said.

There is just something about being part of a winning team, whether it's on a Little League team that just swept the double-header or the parts company that just scored a multi-million dollar contract. We revel in team victory.

And it starts with leadership.

"If a follower can see his or her leader engaged, making sure the team has enough resources to succeed, and celebrating the successes of the team," they are a success, according to Jim Parrish. "We need to model the way."

Alienating people from each other, from other departments, and from leadership is a controlling mechanism that breeds resentment.

"Those without a service attitude are more focused on just getting the work done without thinking about the needs of others," said Donna Brewington. "They are more likely to say, 'It can't be done' than they are to try to find a way to make it happen."

We spend far too much of our time and efforts on the margins, trying to motivate, inspire, and encourage the vital few who need to change their attitude or performance. The result is that the vast majority of those you lead, those who are consistent, are forgotten.

These steady stalwarts should not be forgotten.

ENGAGES IN FORWARD THINKING VERSUS SHORT-SIGHTED IMPULSIVENESS

Knee jerk leaders walk with a limp. They are always banging their joints on the desk any time someone calls or criticizes or suggests. And they are never happy until everyone around them walks with the same limp.

These kinds of leaders are "short-sighted," according to Jack Fite. "They don't invest in the future."

You can spend your time putting out fires, but the hose only goes so far. It will never reach into the future.

"Leaders who are not service oriented never realize the full potential of the team," said Bill Koons. "They often end up with high turnover, lack of commitment, and lack of inspiration."

Measured, patient decisions with the team in mind gather respect.

"Those who have a personal agenda or dictate leadership ultimately divide and tear down individuals or an organization," said Jim Boecker. "They create an underlying anxiety that demotivates. People just leave this kind of environment."

Tough Calls

TOUGH CALLS

WHO WILL STEP UP?

"A pessimist sees the difficulty in every opportunity. An optimist sees the opportunity in every difficulty." – Winston Churchill

One difference between an effective leader and an ineffective leader is the ability to make tough calls. True leaders rise up during adversity and find the impetus and the desire to forge on. Success often hinges on one moment, one call that must be made.

Tough calls have to be made by every leader at some point. They aren't always about personnel, despite the fact that hiring and firing, promotions and demotions, expansion and contraction seem to dominate our landscape.

Tough calls are often about the big picture. At some point, every organization needs to look internally and decide about its direction.

One of the worst traps we can get into is "what used to be." The

THIS CHAPTER'S CONTRIBUTORS
Jere Adcock
Paul Bishop
Charles Borden
Steve Cook
David King
J Allen Meadows
Rebecca Morlando

world is moving at warp speed, and it takes decisiveness to stay ahead of the change.

Modern industry, by nature, is dynamic, not static. Consumer sentiments change. Competitors offer new service or lower their prices to win market share. Events happen that can shake any plan to its core.

If we get stuck on *"what used to be,"* we risk missing out on *"what is."* By making the tough calls, we can fully prepare for *"what will be."*

You might think that your organization is running so well that you'll never have to make these kinds of calls. But the real measure is in a thousand minor decisions you make, and when it's time to make the biggest one of your life, you're ready.

What are the characteristics of a leader who makes tough calls? We turned to our panel of leaders for their insights.

They care about the team over the individual

Jere Adcock relays the difficult decision he has to make when it comes time to part ways with a coach or to sit a player. "It's never easy. And I always pray first," he said. "Most of the time the decisions come down to standards set by our program. Those standards are set for the good of the program."

When you use a standard—those guiding principles we talked about earlier in this book—then it's easier to make tough calls.

"People forfeit their 'right' to be here because they vacated our principles," said Jere.

When you have a core value that guides your team, then nothing should detract you from that.

Charles Borden discussed a difficult decision to terminate an employee who was thirty years his senior. "This individual was a hard worker, but the desired results were not there," he recalls. Despite continued instruction, help, and feedback, the situation didn't improve and Charles had to make that final decision. "His work was pulling the team down."

Think about it. You've spent considerable effort developing a plan and building a team that is engaged. The tough call to separate those people—or situations– that detract from this course is the right thing to do. It shows to those you lead your level of commitment to the vision.

You have to do it not just for the sake of the vision, but for the sake of all those who tossed their own aspirations and doubts to the wind and joined you. Often they've sacrificed their own dreams and plans to join in with the team. One person shouldn't be able to deny the team success.

"The overall health of the organization needs to be considered," offers Paul Bishop.

THEY OVERCOME PREJUDICE, INSTEAD ACTING IN WISDOM

Our brains are amazing repositories of information. We retain hard facts, like the score of our favorite team's final win in the World Series or how many teaspoons of sugar to use in the cookie recipe.

We use these facts as we walk through the woods of our life experiences. We know which paths lead to nowhere—because we've been on them. We also know the rabbit trails that might take us to a destination, but are overgrown and difficult. We also know the main trail, because others have walked it, making it smooth and clear.

That's what wisdom is.

Along the journey we have a steady stream of memories that play like a movie in our brains, flashing when prompted by a current event. We have these retained impressions of people, places, or things. And sometimes, those impressions get in the way.

Making tough calls means cutting through all the clutter of feelings about people, memories of other situations, and personal fears.

J. Allen Meadows had a thirteen-year employee whom he characterized as a "loyal person, productive employee, and a leader."

"She was a partner in our mission, but her personal situation changed and affected her attitude." According to J. Allen, attendance issues, overall dissatisfaction, and negative attitudes began to fester.

"When she had become a toxic influence in our workplace, a change had to be made."

They don't go by feelings or desire, but they do what's right

If you look back at your time in leadership, it's likely been marked by some surprises—twists to your carefully laid plans. And if we are honest, the unexpected should be expected. It happens to the best of us. Markets, competition, personnel, and natural disaster all can knock the ship off course.

When faced with challenges to your organization, the initial response is usually emotional. You're likely to be surprised or even angry. We all deal with situations differently, but I want to encourage you to move quickly past feelings to doing what's right.

The real winners are those who meet these hiccups with resilience and recovery.

Resiliency is the ability to weather any storm. If you add this skill to your tool box, you won't panic or feel overwhelmed when things go awry. A steady demeanor doesn't let emotion interfere with the job at hand. You will feel emotion, and you should if you are human. But to balance that out will help move your team forward.

And then recovery is picking up the pieces and charting a new course. You may not feel like doing anything, and even retreating sounds better at the moment. But tough calls mean that you do what's right even when every fiber in you wants to quit.

THEY SEEK INPUT FROM OTHERS

Steve Cook of Space Technologies Dynetics had a tough call regarding the space program and the development of the Ares IX.

"I gathered my leadership team together and we reviewed the project's scope, benefits, and costs," said Steve. "We debated the merits and issues. While it was ultimately my decision, it was critical to get input from a wide range of interests."

In October 2009, the Ares IX launched on a fully successful mission.

When we talked about ownership early in this book, I emphasized the principle of buy-in. Feedback on the day-to-day operation is easy. But when millions of dollars are at stake, when shareholder's interests are on the line, or when a company's reputation is hanging in the balance, there's no better time to bring in many voices.

It's a tough call to say, "I don't know it all, and I need your help."

THEY ARE WILLING TO TAKE RESPONSIBILITY

When things go wrong, sometimes the first response is to implicate the people behind the situation. While accountability is important, we often get tripped up looking for the guilty party instead of actually fixing the problem.

Ultimately, it doesn't matter whose fault it is. What matters is, where do we go from here?

We live in a world that thrives on finding mistakes instead of creating solutions. If you must affix blame, then do so with a resolution in the other hand.

Usually, those involved sense what needs to be done. A plant needs to close. A boss needs to change. An employee needs to be terminated. A player needs to be benched. There is an unspoken truth that languishes, words that no one dares speak.

The effective leader steps up and takes responsibility. Paul Bishop spoke about an employee he needed to let go. He sensed that a change was needed, but hesitated until other voices supported the change. He made the move and terminated the employee.

"Surprisingly, the affected employee seemed relieved that she was being separated," he said.

What a revealing statement! But it's true. Usually everyone knows what needs to be done—even if it hurts them individually. They just need someone to do it.

"The team was supportive of the change, and immediately a more relaxed atmosphere descended on the work environment," he said. "In the end, the tough call should have been sooner."

THEY TAKE THE APPROPRIATE AMOUNT
OF TIME TO MAKE A DECISION

When we have difficult decisions before us, we tend to handle them one of two ways. We rush into them, just to get them out of the way, or we delay, hoping they'll just go away.

No one likes tough calls, but it's important to take the right amount of time to review the problem, evaluate possible courses of action, and make the prudent decision.

Rebecca Morlando has an interesting observation. She advises to "go slow to go fast." She believes in a deliberate approach that actually speeds along the ultimate decision. "Don't let artificial deadlines drive you to make a decision faster than you need to go."

Sometimes, there's a clock ticking the seconds down. But ask first, "Who set the clock in the first place?" If it can be reset, or delayed, then do what you can to buy a little time.

GATHER THE DATA

Rebecca also advises to take time to gather the data you need. "But don't over analyze it," she said. "Challenge yourself to find the balance between enough and not too much."

There's something about having data, research, and facts on your side. It has a way of swaying the mind that is far too prone to emotional appeals.

Facts can destroy just about anyone if they are twisted in just the right way. There is a time for looking at the facts and another time to examine the heart. And no book or leadership program will tell you when that is. It's simply important for you to know that the moment awaits and you must look for it.

THEY ARTICULATE THE DECISION WITH
SENSITIVITY AND FIRMNESS

By the very nature of "tough" calls, there will be opposition to the final decision. No amount of data gathering, analysis, or team input will soften the blow to those who do not agree.

Your decision can't be given in a capricious manner. The iron fist when unclenched might leave only dust in its wake. However, if you deliver the news with sensitivity, you may still gain respect, even among those who disagree.

David King once took over a large organization that was stale and needed to change in order to survive and grow.

At the center of the stagnation was one person who had served for many years and was well-loved by the workforce. "It was obvious we needed fresh leadership, as the environment had changed," recalled David. "This individual had my utmost respect and had even helped me along in my career."

Tough call? You bet.

"I fretted over this decision for some time, knowing it would mark my leadership in that organization for good or bad. I just needed the courage to do it," he said.

The individual wasn't happy with the decision but, with time, understood the reasoning.

"I was very careful to do it with all dignity and respect toward him," said David. "But it solidified me as a leader who could make the tough calls. And it gained me respect in the end."

And this doesn't just apply to termination. It can also apply to expansion of operations. It can apply to the decision to sell buildings, or move locations, or add new personnel. Just think through the tough calls to those who are affected most, and then with both firmness and sensitivity, be up-front.

Choose your words carefully, and you might just gain their respect.

TOUGH CALLS

BACKBONE OR WISHBONE?

"The real art of conversation is not only to say the right thing at the right time, but also to leave unsaid the wrong thing at the tempting moment." – Dorothy Nevel

So you've made the tough call. You've gathered the data, sought the advice from others, and evaluated all the options. You've arrived at the toughest time in your leadership. But the hard work isn't over until you've actually communicated the tough call.

David King tells us that "people are endeared to someone who has the courage to make tough calls." And he's right. That lump in your throat, the knot in your back, and the pain in your stomach all scream at you to retreat, but true leadership means you have to press on.

I've seen two extremes when communicating tough calls.

1) My way or the highway. We've seen these kinds of leaders, and their bully tactics simply don't work in the long run. But it's a

THIS CHAPTER'S CONTRIBUTORS
Paul Bishop
Charles Borden
Anna Clifton
Steve Cook
David King
Jane Knight
Rebecca Morlando
Mike Stanfield

genuine temptation. When you use this methodology you don't have to explain yourself, justify your position, or have any concern for others. The decision is made.

The problem is that you will have to live with the fallout of this kind of decision-making.

2) I'll let you guess. Believe it or not, many choose to hide their final decision. They let the news roll out through the rumor mill, or the media, or by a whisper campaign. That way, "I never have to face the music." Well, the music does eventually play—and if you wait, it can be deafening.

"There have been times in my leadership when my great idea failed not because of the credibility of the idea, but because of how I communicated it," admits Rebecca Morlando.

And that applies for the hard calls that go along with every great idea. "Sugar-coating this thing only serves as an enabler for some in the organization," said David. "And time doesn't make bad news any better."

It's the time for True Grit to come out. *How are you going to communicate your tough call?*

We asked our leadership panel for their advice.

UNDERSTAND THE GRAVITY OF THE SITUATION

Tough calls usually affect people's lives. If it's on a sport team, you'll cut to the heart of the athlete, impacting his or her perceived ability and dedication to training. If it's in a business, you may shake the pay and security of people who have families. If it's in a volunteer organization, you'll influence the sense of pride and mission of those involved.

"The communication can't stop here," says Mike Stanfield. There are many consequences to any tough decisions. It is my hope that in the end, they are all good and positive. But the truth is, negativity can shroud many tough calls.

It's serious business.

"This is an endeavor which requires much thought and consideration while realizing that you will not make everyone happy," said Paul Bishop. He's right. The very nature of tough calls means that someone will be disappointed. If everyone would be thrilled, it wouldn't be much of a tough call.

So the gravity of the situation means that you should clear the deck of other issues so you can give this your full measure of attention. Those you lead will pay attention to the respect and solemnity you give the situation. If you are glib, or distant, or disconnected, that attitude will be transmitted in only a negative sense.

REALIZE HOW THE MESSAGE MAY BE RECEIVED

In communicating tough calls, realize that everyone has a different receptor. The same words will come out of your mouth, but they will be heard and perceived in a variety of ways.

I once worked for what I call "a straight shooter." There was no dance in his lingo, no gray in his color palette, and no twilight in his day. It was black and white all the way. After a while, I grew to understand his approach and even appreciated the frank talk. I always knew where I stood. Other employees were put off by the bluntness. They needed a little bread in their meat sandwich.

You have to think about the words you use, your mannerism, and your style. Hopefully, you have others who can speak truth into your life and tell you how you're perceived. You can then make adjustments so your style doesn't interfere with the message.

Deliver with Compassion and Determination

Delivering tough communication is almost a learned trait. I would love for you to be able to take these few words and come out an expert. You won't, because it's just not that easy. It's a trial-and-tribulation process that is marked more by what you do wrong than what you do right.

"As I have matured and gained experience, I now better understand that I need to be empathetic and steadfast at the same time," reflects Paul Bishop.

Too many of us think that being the boss is all about making decisions and then carrying them out "come hell or high water." Many young leaders, looking to establish territory and make an impression, fall into this trap.

Compassion can be carried out at the same time as determination.

This kind of balance is a start-to-finish process, according to Anna Clifton. "The leader must stay involved by supporting teammates,

> "Compassion can be carried out at the same time as determination."

getting and giving feedback, and making adjustments when necessary. And giving continuous communication shows the leader's character and integrity."

Allow for Input from All Parties Involved

In communicating the tough call, you might be tempted to just deliver the news and duck out. But that would negate your team and put everyone into the hierarchal role that you've tried so hard to change.

There has to be some time for people to respond. They need a chance to ask questions, to vent and to have a voice. It may be painful and uncomfortable, but it's a necessary part of long-term health for both your organization and for them as individuals.

And don't let the tough call be a surprise to other leadership. They need to be involved as well, even if indirectly. That way, they can provide necessary input and support.

CREATE PUBLIC AND PRIVATE CONVERSATIONS

If you are in charge of a big operation, you're going to have to make some decisions about how to deliver the tough news. It might be that your company didn't get a contract. It might be that the plant is downsizing. It might be the replacement of a key leader. These things tend to leak out in very quick order unless you deliver the news rapidly and publicly.

"If adequate information has been provided up-front and if the potentially impacted parties have been given warnings, the communication of a tough decision is much easier," reminds Charles Borden. "But the need for privacy may preclude the ability to provide up-front information."

We live in a world that thrives on leaks and information, thanks to Twitter, Facebook and the blogosphere. Rarely can you keep news under wraps for long. So gather the team, step up to the microphone, and speak the hard truth.

Afterwards, you need to meet with as many small groups as possible to answer questions, to allay concerns, and to go into more in-depth conversations. And there will be people you will need to meet with in private. All of this should be done in the shortest time frame possible to avoid any kind of misunderstandings.

Mike Stanfield believes in the personal touch. You should never delegate these kinds of discussions. "This should include as many personal conversations as possible," he said. "Any mass communications should be personally written by the leader."

KNOW HOW MUCH TO DISCLOSE

You may not know or be able to share all the details, so be honest in what you talk about and what you cannot disclose. Those who follow you can handle some uncertainty, but when sweeping changes are occurring and they hear nothing from you, your credibility and authority are undermined.

The direction, strength, and hope you offer will stand the test of time.

"There are a lot of things that can be said one-on-one, or in small groups, that can't be done in a mass communication," said David King.

Jane Knight had some difficult information to deliver, but it had to be done over several weeks. "For the sake of the vision, I delivered it to the clients I served directly first," she said. "Then, I gave it to my team leader and then with her guidance shared it with the rest of the team. We chose a gradual delivering of information, knowing this allowed us time to carefully consider options."

USE WRITTEN SCRIPTS IF THEY ARE HELPFUL

Usually, communicating tough calls are equal parts passion and emotion. First you have zeal to get things fixed, a certain adrenaline that goes with leadership through crisis. And there's the emotional and physical energy associated with making the leap. Meanwhile, there are those doubts, the lingering naysaying that whispers in your ear.

David King doesn't go into these situations without enough time to create a plan on what he'll say. "Being thoughtful about a communications plan for any tough call is paramount in gaining acceptance."

Rebecca Morlando goes a step further. "Now I've learned to write down a formal communication plan."

A formal communication plan gives the background for the decision, a script for stand-up talks or face-to-face conversations, press releases, and a list of anticipated questions and answers.

Obviously, a small organization or team wouldn't need all of this, but the components are important to note. What will the opposition say? Can you answer every question about the decision? What can you say legally? Do you have facts and background readily available?

If you have all of this homework done, you can walk into tough communications situations with tremendous confidence. When you develop this written script and associated material, you'll likely have to engage the help of others who can act as advisors and confidants. When you deliver the message, you are delivering on behalf of all of them.

Mike Stanfield has a simple checklist. "Explain the situation and what we face, why the decision was made, and the impact on the company and the staff."

DON'T DEBATE ONCE YOU HAVE MADE THE DECISION

Getting input and feedback from others is one thing, but debating is something entirely different. Any differences or disagreement should happen in private, not publicly.

> "It should be obvious that a change is coming because the values are so strong that the status quo stands opposed to them."

Steve Cook has been able to deliver good news over his twenty-five years of leadership and as Director of Space Technologies at Dynetics. But he's had to deliver plenty of bad news, too—lost contracts, test failures, downsizing, and changes in mission by the

U.S. Government. But one thing he has learned is to not blame others, but to deliver the message in "unambiguous terms."

"It must be made clear to the team that there is a time for debate and discussion," he said. "But, absent new and compelling data, once the decision is made, the team moves forward to execute."

When people continually have freedom to debate decisions, "it's a momentum killer, costing key resources," Steve said.

SHARE THE VALUES THAT DROVE YOUR DECISION

If you have established a goal, and if you've communicated the values that encase that goal, then delivering tough news shouldn't be a surprise. In other words, it should be obvious to everyone that a change is coming because the values are so strong that the status quo stands opposed to them.

"Every good leader works to tell their story, expressing the ideas, values, and emotional energy involved in making a call," said Anna Clifton.

Your organizations' story has a beginning—back to when that first vision was cast. And it has a hook, when everyone believed and made the mission their own. And the story has multiple chapters. Some are adventures. Some are comedic in nature. And some are tragic.

"One should define why the change was necessary, what the next steps are, how those actions will be accomplished, and what it will take to get there," said Anna.

Tough calls aren't the end of the story. They are part of the plotline that gets to the grand finale. And if you have an overarching theme—a place where you want the story to end—you should communicate this to those you lead, even if it's difficult.

TOUGH CALLS

THE COURAGE TO ACT

"Success is not final. Failure is not fatal. It's the courage to continue that counts." – Winston Churchill

It's easy to be a leader in the good times. What's not to like? The achievements, the rewards, and the accolades are easy to ingest. The praise from senior leadership feels good, your customers like you, and employees all share in the success.

But when things aren't going well, everything changes. The victories are few and far between. The criticism mounts. Everything starts falling apart one thing at a time. Like a dammed wall, the leaks start coming and you just don't know where the next one will show.

THIS CHAPTER'S CONTRIBUTORS

Robert Aderholt
Jere Adcock
Paul Bishop
Steve Cook
Mike Stanfield
David King

If you just wait, your organization will be overwhelmed by a swamp of negativity.

But a courageous leader is intentional—and has to be more than present. He or she needs to be actively engaged with those they lead. True leaders rise up during adversity and provide the impetus and the desire to survive, if not thrive.

Sometimes leaders have to deliver bad news—and that takes courage. The road to recovery is a long, hard one that's uncertain at best. Courage isn't just desire. It's heart, and that's a tough thing for hard, driving leaders to absorb from our current culture.

What is the mark of someone with the courage to act? We asked our leadership panel to tell us, and this is what they said:

THEY CAN SEE THE BIG PICTURE

It seems that great leaders somehow have a way of seeing into the future. They can understand trends, challenges, and the bumps in the road. What is it about these men and women?

> "True leaders rise up during adversity and provide the impetus and the desire to survive, if not thrive."

They have the courage to see the big picture. Small-minded people have an obsession with the present. They see monsters behind every shadow, threats in every communication, and danger around every corner.

And there are those who are always "safe," so they'll never engage in seeing the big picture because it might involve change. And change to these people must "be avoided at all costs."

"I think the toughest calls are those where a leader has a vision that is clear to them, but a little fuzzy to others, "observes David King. He recalls a manager who took a big step to build a facility that acted as a showcase for products. He did it when demand for the products was in decline. "But that decision redefined us," said David. "Without that step, we would have lost ground and shrunk."

One of the most significant indicators of both corporate and individual success is great expectations. When you start the day looking at the big picture and planning for success, others will follow. If you walk in thinking small, then you probably will fail. And others will emulate. They'll follow your expectations.

THEY ARE WILLING TO DO THE RIGHT THING

When a tough call needs to be made, those you lead know deep inside what that call needs to be.

They see the landscape, understand the challenges, and likely see the obstacles. One by one, they turn their hearts and their eyes to you and the others that lead your organization. They all ask, "Will he do the right thing? Will she make the right choice?"

By choosing the right thing, you may very well sacrifice the future of your organization.

I love what Albert Einstein said: "Relativity applies to physics, not ethics." For every wrong reason there is a very compelling argument. But in the end, they are simply justifications.

Jere Adcock remembers his father, a grocer. In 1970, he hired an African-American to be a visible part of the front of his store in the Deep South. Despite boycotts, negative comments, and testy situations, his dad stood his ground. "This young man will stay, but you can take your business elsewhere."

This comment, before racial attitude adjustments, likely cost him money and status. But it was the right thing to do. "His stand and compassion was one of the strongest memories of leadership I ever experienced," said Jere.

If it's a tough call, you will be ridiculed. There will be those who will stand on the sidelines and wag their heads, throwing down money betting on your demise. Stand tall. *Prove them wrong.*

Humorist Mark Twain gave some simple advice. "Always do right—this will gratify some and astonish the rest."

They Don't Act Out of Selfish Motives

As a nation, we've seen executives pad their estates just before a company goes down. We've seen others resign just before an investigation, letting someone else take the heat. We've observed it in our own lives, as the will to survive often tries to nudge out our sense of right and wrong.

The abolitionist Wendell Phillips said, "Physical bravery is an animal instinct; moral bravery is much higher and truer courage."

Self-preservation is a powerful instinct, but acting out

> "For every wrong reason there is a very compelling argument. But in the end, they are simply justifications."

of courage means resisting that protectionist urge. Those you lead will understand self-preservation, but they will never respect it.

If you ask your team to sacrifice money, standing, or security, you should lead in the sacrifice.

"It is very courageous to lay aside your personal interests and wants and put the entire organization ahead of yourself," said Paul Bishop. "As leaders, we always need to try to put others before us."

I think of George Bailey in *It's a Wonderful Life*. As his savings and loan began to experience a rush on deposits, he dipped in his own wallet to begin paying those demanding cash. When the depositors saw his sacrifice, they modified their own need for self-preservation.

His personal interests took a back seat to the corporate good of his friends and neighbors.

Viktor Frankl, who lived through the Nazi concentration camps, remembers the few men who walked through huts comforting others, giving away their last piece of bread.

"They offer sufficient proof that everything can be taken from a man, but one thing: the last of human freedoms—to choose one's attitude in any set of circumstances, to choose one's own way."

The first act of courage starts with the man or woman in the mirror.

THEY DISPLAY CONFIDENCE IN THE FACE OF UNCERTAINTY

Steve Cook likes to tell the story of General Dwight Eisenhower and his decision to invade Normandy in June 1944. Despite tremendous uncertainty, "he stood confident," Steve said.

Gen. Eisenhower had to make the decision to launch thousands of planes and ships and move 160,000 troops across the English Channel.

The timetable was set for a few select days in early June 1944, but terrible weather moved in. Such a large-scale operation in bad conditions was certain to cost lives, but waiting for better weather could extend the war for years. Day after day, the forecasters briefed the General with the same bad news. But on June 5, meteorologists predicted a narrow sliver of a break in the weather for the next day.

The meteorologists weren't certain. After all, it was the weather. But Eisenhower took the chance and confidently made the decision to invade that evening.

"If I let any of my commanders think that maybe things weren't going to work out, that I was afraid, they'd be afraid too," said General Eisenhower. "I had to have the confidence. I had to make them believe that everything was going to work out."

> "People won't follow wishy-washy. They will, however, follow courage."

I'm not advocating dishonesty. And you should always be clear about the possibility of failure, but courage to proceed will inspire others.

There is something I call the Pied Piper Effect. If you play loud enough, long enough, and with confidence, you'll inspire others to follow you.

People won't follow wishy-washy. They will, however, follow courage.

TAKE PERSONAL RESPONSIBILITY

"Ultimately, the decision was mine." Whenever I see a statement like this on the evening news, I have to smile. It definitely goes against the current blame game. How rare it is to see men and women step up into the responsibility of leadership.

I remember the first job I had as a supervisor. It was at a family-owned fast food restaurant. I was a shift leader. They gave me ten cents extra an hour, the keys to the back door, and a stern warning that I was responsible. When someone slipped carrying out the trash, I was responsible. When someone didn't show for their shift, I was responsible. When someone gave out too much change, I was responsible.

I didn't always think this was fair. After all, I wasn't the one who performed the irresponsible actions. But my mother told me that with titles—even if the pay didn't reflect it – comes responsibility and I would have to step into it.

Sometimes we feel the responsibility isn't worth the hassle. And it isn't for everyone.

Depending on what you lead, you probably have a key or two that no one else has. Those keys are both a real and a symbolic sign of your responsibility. They can unlock physical doors, but you also have the responsibility to unlock the potential of your unit. And that's heavy duty stuff.

Some will give away their keys, or leave them home, neglecting the responsibility. But if you properly use them, you can unlock the outlook of your entire team.

So the next time you turn a lock or swipe a badge, think about responsibility.

Don't delegate the hard decisions to others

Mike Stanfield recalls a situation where he watched the president of his company deal with a difficult decision. A couple of group leaders were resigning, taking a number of other team members with them.

"Instead of compromising, the president himself escorted the employees out of the premises," said Mike. There was fallout, as these people had relationships with customers. The president called them himself and explained the situation.

"Instead of compromising company integrity, he and the other leaders chose to accept potential consequences of lost business," said Mike.

In the following days, those that remained were dealt with honestly and respectfully. The team rallied around the hard call of the leadership and gathered the resources to meet the customers' needs.

"They were committed to the core principles of building a company of integrity and excellence," said Mike. "I believe it worked."

You can't make hard calls from a corner office, or a coach's office, or from corporate headquarters and let others communicate them. You can't communicate from a distance and expect any respect or growth.

They lead with maturity

Finger-pointing is one of the classic signs of immaturity at any stage of life. When I was a boy, I would lift a voice of protest to my little brother whenever I got in trouble, making him complicit.

As an adult, this kind of behavior is more subtle, but often the same. We look for others to blame, offer excuses for situations, or find ways to squirm out of difficult decisions.

I've seen cities point their fingers at other communities for their own crime rates, executives blame workers for laziness, and spouses accuse the other of communication breakdowns.

On the other hand, mature leaders identify problems, honestly evaluate them, and move to fix them. If others are affected, engaging them in the resolution helps move things along more quickly.

The tongue can be a fire, as we see evidenced in the world around us. And I have dropped my fair share of sparks through words that weren't quite well-thought-out before I spoke them. Impulsiveness has its moments, and sometimes decisions just have to be made on the spot. But a thoughtful, measured approach is the better path.

They put others' interests first

Those who simply follow leaders because they are afraid of discipline or because it is expected, often do so half-heartedly. Their dispassionate efforts are all part of a lifelong sentence to the chain gang, going through the motions.

When people act this way, it's because they are simply working for the machine, working for "the man." No wonder they aren't engaged and committed. However, if you put their interests above your own, suddenly the tables are turned.

"If you don't appreciate the privileges you have been given, then it's difficult to lead in such a way that you can be mindful of the needs of others," observes Congressman Robert Aderholt

As we've seen, courage is equal parts bravery and humility. Find the right mix and you'll change your organization, if not the world.

HEALTH

HEALTH MATTERS

LEADERSHIP VERTIGO

"By improving yourself, the world is made better. Be not afraid of growing too slowly. Be afraid only of standing still." -Ben Franklin

A "healthy" lifestyle means different things to different people. In fact, the bookstore neatly puts lifestyle titles into helpful categories. The psychology and self-help section encourages readers to change the way they think, evaluate how they feed their mental state, and manage a balanced outlook toward others.

The body and wellness section of the bookstore has book jackets graced with cover photos of tape measures, fit models, and natural glowing skin. Good diets, regular exercise, and outdoor activity are all tenets of these books.

The spiritual section has religious guidance from the East

THIS CHAPTER'S CONTRIBUTORS

Gary Abney
Paul Bishop
Terri Collins
John Dupes
Larry Hyche
Kelly Jackson
John Knight
Kristy Knight
Greg Lester
Rebecca Morlando
Ian Poulton
Bobby Welch

to the West and everywhere in between. They speak to the deeper things, the soul matters that we cannot measure.

Which one makes for great leaders? Short answer? *They all do.*

Healthy leaders take care of themselves and understand the connection between soul, body, and mind. You can't be unhealthy personally and still lead an organization. A healthy leader has the ability to understand that their personal health is paramount to success.

Healthy leaders are also relational. "Nothing is more fulfilling on this earth than having healthy relationships with family and friends," said NFL linebacker Reggie Torbor. "It's the reason we are all here. Work is last because it's the least stable of all these things. The worst moments in my life have been when work crept up my priority list."

We turned to our leadership panel to get their take. We asked them about their *successes—and failures*—in maintaining a healthy, balanced life.

ESTABLISH PRIORITIES

Passionate people tend to get involved—and over involved. They see every dim light as a grand opportunity for a beacon and every possibility is a probability to change the world.

"Passion to succeed often takes a front seat to many other aspects of a leader's life—family, friends, recreation," said John Dupes. "It's a dangerous cocktail that can create adverse effects. I made the effort to prioritize my time and attention, and in doing so, my drive didn't disappear. It actually thrived in all areas."

If you find yourself stretched with all good and noble things, you are probably drinking from the cocktail John talks about.

The answer is to find a few things and do them well.

"You have to establish priorities and be committed to them," said Bobby Welch. "You won't be 100 percent successful every day, but the pattern of your life should reflect those priorities."

"My success has come from prioritizing," said John Knight. "It's being disciplined with time management. My struggles have come from not understanding how much is 'too much.'"

INVOLVE SELF-DISCIPLINE

There has never been such a time as this, when our leisure activities are limitless, our involvement with humanitarian pursuits varied, and our options for entertainment at the click of button anywhere, anytime.

Part of the industrial revolution was to free men and women from the drudgery of everyday chores. No one has to beat their clothes on rocks or gather firewood for cooking these days. But all that freedom simply got filled in with other things, and we have never felt more trapped.

"I can't tell you how many ball games, dance recitals, date nights, and social invitations I missed due to my insatiable desire to succeed," admits John Dupes.

He couldn't say no, because he was so engaged. And that's what leaders often do. But self-discipline means saying no, even to worthwhile things.

"Sure there are days when I have to work late or make a weekend visit to the office," admits Bobby Welch. "But overall, work will not take priority or dominate my life."

UNDERSTAND BOUNDARIES

For a book designer, margin is an important design element. If you were reading this book and the words filled every square inch of the printed page, your pupils couldn't focus. You wouldn't be able to comprehend the concepts or the meaning, because your mind's eye would be stressed and tired from the overload.

It's the same with our lives. We need margin, a little white space with nothing in it.

"For me, that means not working on weekends or on vacations," said Bobby. "I attend my kids' activities and I'm available to my family," he said. "Time means love to them, and I only have a limited amount before they are grown and gone."

Some are able to draw strong boundaries to help protect that white space. Personally, I believe that line should be less in bold strokes and more dotted. Let me explain. I have a friend who refuses to discuss work at home. But the problem with this approach is that your involvement with your job, team, or organization is a big part of your life—a huge part. And those that love us and care about us need to be involved somehow.

For years I have started the dinner conversation with the question, "What's the most interesting thing you did today?" And for those of us working, that meant stories about coworkers, projects, customers, and challenges.

I think healthy integration, rather than disengagement, is a better approach.

But there's a limit. And there should be a time and a place for everything. Establish some boundaries and stick to them. The boundaries may involve e-mail, phone calls, or paperwork. There has to be some time when you do not allow any of this to encroach on your family or personal time. Let others know what the boundaries are and ask them to hold you accountable. They'll appreciate your efforts and reward you with respect.

Ian Poulton has three rules. "I can't work on the weekends unless the family agrees. I don't bring any work home. And I try to stay with a fixed work schedule." This may not be practical for everyone, but those are the boundaries he needs.

Larry Hyche's struggle is with the telephone. "When I am home, I don't carry my cell phone around with me. It sits on the counter. If I don't hear it because I am outside, then I don't answer it," he said. "Texts, tweets, e-mails, and calls could dominate anyone's day if allowed."

Your personal time needs boundaries as well. There is only one you. And you need to eat right, exercise, worship, play, and sometimes just do nothing. Boundaries help protect all of that.

I can't tell you what those boundaries look like for you, but if you ask those closest to you, they'll have a pretty good idea how to get you started.

You need to establish boundaries in your relationships with those you lead, too. When Kelly Jackson took over a plant maintenance operation, he realized that it ran round-the-clock—and so did the problems. "When I first took the job, I was often the first point of contact when there were equipment issues, and the expectation was that I show up, at any hour, to provide resolution."

That didn't last long. He wisely set up a structure which gave others authority to make decisions without an obligatory call to the boss. "They are empowered to resolve the issues at hand," said Kelly. "I still get midnight and weekend calls, but their occurrence has decreased dramatically. This has improved my outlook."

DIVERSIFY YOUR INVOLVEMENT

Some advocate a balanced and healthy lifestyle by subtraction. Reduce the number of engagements, beg out of commitments, and eliminate anything that is absolutely unnecessary.

It's true that many of us have no business being involved in certain things. I remember once—at the height of my insane schedule—I said yes to judge a Girl Scout bake-off. Not having any children in the program made me an outsider, but they thought I could be funny and provide a sense of leadership at the competition.

I had no business being there. I was trying to lose weight (and I had to sample all thirty-one plates just to be fair). It took away my only night of the week with my family, and it did nothing to improve my life or anyone else's. I went out of obligation and pride, because it made me feel good that I was honored with such a task.

But simply looking for baking contests to wipe out is really not the answer. Leaders should be involved in many things on many fronts. If you have the gift of leadership, you will be involved with your organization, your church, your neighborhood, and your community at large. It goes with the territory.

"While reducing the number of involvements is sometimes a practical necessity," said Greg Lester, "the ability to lead effectively is enhanced by broad experiences and diversity of perspective."

What Greg is saying is that you will be a better leader in your organization if you diversify your gifts. Something kicks the brain into overdrive when you are engaged in different aspects of life.

"A requirement for balance produces an engaging, thoughtful, and satisfying leadership," said Greg.

BE INTENTIONAL

Sometimes all of this just comes together, but usually, it needs to be a purposeful journey.

"Be intentional about scheduling and prioritizing the most important items," advises Paul Bishop. "Then fill in with the lesser things."

The problem is, "everything becomes important." You've seen it in your life. How can you say "no" to Girl Scouts trying to raise money? How can you say "no" to the boss who signs your paycheck? How can you say "no" to church activities that have impact beyond the moment? How can you say "no" to family?

It's all important—to someone. But is it important to you? "Something has to give," said Paul.

That's why intentionality is so vital; otherwise, the creep will overwhelm you. Stick to your vision, your goals, and the direction of your life. And then pick those things that most have an impact on you and your sphere of influence, and throw yourself into them.

"Review the things which are most important to you at the current time," said Paul. But don't get stuck in those things, because "each of us goes through 'seasons,' where different aspects of our life become more or less important."

"It's hard to make these choices in the heat of the moment," observes Rebecca Morlando. "Make them in advance based on your values. Then tell those that are important in your life what your plan is and ask for their support in reaching your goal."

Part of Gary Abney's balance is found in relationships with others. "I am part of a group of men who mentor each other. I find healing for my own weaknesses and meaning in life as I pass on to others what I can to help them be all they can be," he said.

APPRECIATE HUMOR

At the end of the day, unless your team is defusing a nuclear bomb or stopping an asteroid, there's always tomorrow. What you are doing can usually be repaired if it's done wrong.

It's okay to laugh a little—to even chuckle at your own weakness. Ian Poulton says this is part of "being a human. Get a sense of humor." When you lead others and you do so with a quick laugh on your lips, you'll instantly be granted access. You still have to earn the rest with competence, but a quick retort, an off-the-cuff remark, or a laugh will give you a great head start.

Find a way to nurture your laughable side. Rent the movie

Airplane! Read the funnies on Sunday. Have lunch with the office jokester. Whatever you do, just learn to laugh a little.

Even in adversity there can be a moment of levity. If you make the best of the bad, you'll laugh about it in the future. And why wait? Start laughing now.

CHOOSE TO MAKE HEALTH A DAILY ENDEAVOR

Maintaining a healthy outlook isn't a singular venture that you can pencil into a planner. It's a way of life, a daily endeavor. "It begins within your heart and your desire. It's the life priorities in the daily choices I make," observes Terri Collins.

"Maintaining a healthy balance is a daily challenge," said Bobby Welch. "You have to establish priorities and be committed to them."

It starts with some disciplines that begin each day: a morning walk, prayer or meditation, reading a book that isn't about work or your organization, talking with family. These things must be built into your everyday if you want to be healthy.

"We all have the same twenty-four hours in every day. How we choose to use them is the difference," said Terri Collins. "*I choose* to start with devotion. *I choose* to include walks. *I choose* to limit some activities."

UNDERSTAND THE IMPORTANCE OF
INTEGRATING TIME MANAGEMENT

Time management is an issue with those living in an unhealthy environment. They can't ever seem to get ahead.

There are hundreds of tools out there: day planners, smart phone applications, and desktop helpers. There are systems, planning books, and processes to help people get ahold of the clock that just seems to run fast.

For me, it's often as simple as a numbered yellow notepad.

"Just because you leave the office doesn't mean your phone won't ring during the night with a crisis or a need," said Kristy Knight. "However, there are things I responded to in the past that I could have left at work."

She's learning to leave behind, go home, and "pick up where I left off the next day."

Tyranny of the Urgent! is a dandy little pamphlet by Charles Hummel. He talks about how the **urgent** things push out the **important** things in our lives. How true.

We should all strive for the most important things in our lives with full vigor, enthusiasm, and effort. This is a healthy leader.

HEALTH MATTERS

THE HEARTBEAT OF A LEADER

"There are no great limits to personal growth because there are no limits of human intelligence, imagination, and wonder." – Ronald Reagan

If you've ever worked in a toxic environment, you know what a drag that can be. It can wreak havoc on your confidence, and generally fosters a sense of malaise. Your passion is gone and you find that you are just putting in time— an endless march, day in, day out.

And worse, unhealthy environments are like a virus. They infect, spread, and grow, one person at a time. "Unhealthy leadership goes from person to person, destroying their potential," observes Rebecca Morlando. "The negative impact on an organization is viral and can incapacitate it."

But she has a vaccine to an

unhealthy environment: healthy leadership. "By modeling the right behaviors, you can prepare every individual to fight 'the virus' resulting in an effective organization," she said.

"People thrive under healthy leadership," Kristy Knight said. "They will accept responsibility and want to be held accountable. But unhealthy leadership causes distrust and a lack of confidence."

Unfortunately, we are better at describing unhealthy leaders than healthy leaders. Everyone, it seems, has a story about a bad boss, coach, or supervisor.

So *what are the marks of a healthy leader?* We turned to our panel of leaders, and here's what they said.

HAVE A VIGOROUS SELF-AWARENESS

Good leaders who lead from a healthy perspective are *self-aware*. We all know people who are completely *self-absorbed*, and this is entirely different. Self-awareness is the ability to perceive your strengths and weaknesses and the associated emotions that go with each character trait.

"You cannot lead others if you don't both understand yourself and have the ability to control yourself," said Mike Stanfield.

Once you have yourself figured out, then you can also understand why others react the way they do. As a young man in my mid-twenties, I was put in charge of about ninety employees, and all but one of them was older. Most were at least twice as old as I was.

How did they perceive me? *Young. Inexperienced. Naive.* And every perception was correct. But for some reason I was chosen to be in charge. I still had a job to do.

Knowing their mistrust of someone so young, I didn't rule with arrogance, but with an attitude of learning. I gave fewer orders and asked more questions like, "How would you solve this problem?" I worked hard to be competent in my job, growing in knowledge and wisdom.

After a while the older guys accepted me, helped me, and even respected me. The biggest reason was because the pants I wore were the right size. They weren't too big. They weren't too small. I knew who I was and didn't try to be anyone different.

"A healthy leader must be aware of his insecurities and weaknesses," said Kelly Jackson. "He does this so he can effectively draw from and utilize the strengths of those around him."

It's not smart to do the books if you are a word guy. If you're not attentive to details, then don't pretend to perform quality assurance. If you aren't a people person, have someone else answer customer calls.

If you work into your strengths and are honest about your weaknesses, you allow others the opportunity to fill the gap with their own abilities. Then they can shine and succeed.

CARE FOR OTHERS AND BE RELATIONAL

A healthy leader is less focused on his or her health and more focused on the health of others. When you have genuine concern for your peers, subordinates, and superiors in your organization, you'll end up with a healthy outlook for yourself.

"A healthy leader is one that takes care of themselves, their family, and maintains relationships with friends," said Terri Collins. "A healthy leader cares about those people they represent and lead."

According to Rep. Collins, an atmosphere that is "supportive and encouraging of people" is a healthy one. On the other hand, an atmosphere filled with "unattainable goals, little recognition, and no gratitude results in misery and unproductive leadership."

Greg Lester had an unfortunate situation where a competitor was luring away a contributor to one of his teams. But the team member didn't handle the situation properly, openly asking for equal compensation. And he displayed an "attitude shift that was disrupting the work environment."

Rather than meet the money demand, Greg let the disruptive employee go and distributed the raise he was asking to other stalwart team members. "This pulled all of the drama out of the environment."

"Our chemistry was not healthy." He cared about the team enough to take care of the one thing that threatened it.

> "The days of blind allegiance to an organization are long gone. We crave immediate feedback, and we need our leaders to give it to us."

BE AN ENCOURAGER

At the end of a life, there will be no greater honor than to see a line of people you have inspired, encouraged, and brought out the best in so they could succeed.

"Healthy leaders look to equip and empower those who work under them," said Larry Hyche. "They want others to succeed and shine. They use their wisdom in a way that inspires those under them."

This principle is illustrated on the football field. Every position has a backup. In the event of injury or diminished skills, someone is always ready and eager to step in. The smart players, as they age, recognize their time has come, and they begin the peaceful transition. They do everything they can to mentor and school their replacements.

We should do the same thing in our professional lives.

But a funny thing happens along the way. We get jealous. We guard our turfs. We protect our institutional knowledge, our reputation, and our experience. An unhealthy leader is "at the center of his or her world and will squash anyone who tries to take the spotlight away from them. They want to be hero of every story," Larry said.

And Andrew Smith tells us that healthy leaders "think about the future and what could be." They imagine the possibilities and "encourage others to participate and work together" toward that vision.

People need to know that what they do matters. How many people swipe their timecard at the end of the day without hearing a single word of direction, encouragement, or motivation? The days of blind allegiance to an organization are long gone. We crave immediate feedback, and we need our leaders to give it to us.

LEAD FROM CORE VALUES

Strong leaders don't lead from the gut, or from trends, or even the marketplace. They lead from their principles, their core.

Reggie Torbor observes, "Strong foundation equals strong life." According to Reggie, his foundation is a relationship with God, his family, and his friends.

As a professional athlete he also has to keep his "instrument" in tune, with regular workouts and conditioning. Reggie is also careful not to abuse his body, because he has made a commitment to play football to the best of his abilities.

"Healthy leaders lead from the inside out," said Gary Abney.

Your personal mission will likely be different than your corporate or organizational mission. But the two missions should integrate with certain

> "Strong leaders don't lead from the gut, or from trends, or even the marketplace. They lead from their principles, their core."

values. Consistency in integrity and hard work improve every individual and every organization.

For Mike Stanfield, it comes down to one word. "Honesty— It's the basis of trust and along with openness prevents festering of problems and resentment that leads to unhealthy leadership."

LISTEN AND LEARN

It's one thing to take instruction from your boss. It's another to take a hint from a peer. But to take a criticism or suggestion from someone you lead takes a big person. If you go into your job with the right mix of confidence and humility, you'll realize that while you might master a few things, you'll never be able to perfect everything.

You'll stumble. You'll fall. You'll fail.

Being honest with yourself means you are open to the opinions, attitudes, and instruction from others. Andrew Smith has an interesting observation. "Consider that you have failed to lead before assuming someone has failed to follow."

So do you listen? "A healthy leader spends more time listening than talking," said Bobby Welch.

It was said that Eleanor Roosevelt could carry on an entire conversation without ever uttering the word "I." She didn't waste her valuable communication time with tales of her adventure, her opinions, or her persuasion. Instead, she asked questions, listened, and learned.

DISPLAY HUMILITY

Rebecca Morlando seeks to "lead out of humility." This is a powerful stance.

Take the time to step back, out of the limelight. A humble

leader avoids the accolades, gladly letting others get the glory. This kind of leader works hard and is practical in everyday efforts. This genuine leader will eventually gain respect that is far beyond the temporary praise that might come to a proud leader.

Ian Poulton suggests leaders "become human beings first." He's half joking, but it becomes a serious statement when you start to recall some of the leaders you've experienced who didn't know the first thing about what makes people tick. I guarantee the "humanity-deprived" leaders were also proud people. "Once you figure out how to be a human, leadership will follow," said Ian.

Albert Schweitzer was a brilliant young man, but he eschewed several promising careers to spend his life working among Africa's lepers. He was the model of heroic leadership yet deflected any praise.

Schweitzer wrote that he must be "content with small and obscure deeds."

Even when he won the Nobel Peace prize in 1952, Schweitzer used the funds to build a facility to treat lepers. He also wrote that praise from people, institutions, and associations "are like the foam on the waves of a deep ocean."

What will last? *Humility*. It invests in others, in higher purposes, and in goals that far outlive your personal efforts.

Display confidence

"A healthy leader should be able to see the finish line at all times," said Reggie Torbor. "It's confidence. Your team can detect whether you have it or not within a matter of minutes after you stand in front of them."

I've struggled with this concept. I want to be humble and accessible, to not come across as a know-it-all. But confidence is a different animal.

"Confidence is gained by knowledge, study, and due diligence.

Know your team's strengths and weaknesses," said Reggie. "Leading without doing your homework is arrogance. And they will constantly look for a better way than yours."

Confidence is gained and displayed in the smallest of things, those faithful nuggets of decisiveness that create greatness.

Bruce Barton, who built a major ad agency and later served in Congress, ended his time on this earth as an introspective writer. He said, "Sometimes, when I consider what tremendous consequences come from little things—a chance word, a tap on the shoulder, or a penny dropped on a newsstand—I am tempted to think there are no little things."

From the little things, confident leaders with equally confident followers are made.

BE ABLE TO SAY "NO" AS WELL AS "YES"

"A healthy leader has the ability to prioritize and has the ability to say 'no,'" said John Dupes. This is a tough word for many to utter, because we think it's our duty to be involved in every decision.

"If you don't say 'no,' one morning you'll wake up with an overwhelming sense of defeat," according to John.

He's right. You can only be successful at so many things. And when you are overextended, you'll find that many things will turn from successful to unsuccessful in a short amount of time. "If I'm spread too thin, it can easily set the stage for failure," said John.

But on the other hand, if you say "no" to everything, you might just miss out on the opportunity to grow, or to enrich someone else, or to find your calling in life.

"Healthy leadership knows when to go all in," said John. "And it knows when to step back. Not every battle is to be fought."

Too often, leaders retreat to the back room, or to the lawyer's suite, or to the coach's office. If you make the decision, stand tall and announce it. Be bold. Be courageous. If you communicate the decision clearly and confidently you'll win respect. If you let the rumor mill announce it and others define it, then you'll lose in the end.

It needs to be done with just the right balance of sensitivity and firmness—not always an easy task. Spend some time writing out how the message will be delivered. And ask trusted advisors on how it will be perceived. Their inclusiveness in the communication will give you the right words, the right heart, and the right message.

HEALTH

RX FOR CHANGE

"We plant seeds that will flower as results in our lives, so best to remove the weeds of anger, avarice, envy and doubt, that peace and abundance may manifest for all." - Dorothy Day

If you are in any kind of leadership position, people perceive you in many different roles. You can probably list how you are perceived: Motivator, Facilitator, Peacemaker, and many others.

THIS CHAPTER'S CONTRIBUTORS
Gary Abney
Paul Bishop
John Dupes
Larry Hyche
Kelly Jackson
Kristy Knight
Rebecca Morlando
Ian Poulton
Mike Stanfield
Thomas Watson
Bobby Welch

But let's be honest. The role you are usually expected to fulfill is *Fixer.*

Much of what you do on a daily basis is fixing things. In fact, you might believe that's your job—to fix breakdowns, to fix the schedule, to fix the product flow, to fix the delivery. It's a common leadership trait to thrive on chaos and calamity. Some will even create chaos just so they can implement their own solution.

But you will never see long-term success if your organization jumps from crisis to crisis. The tail cannot wag the dog. You have to get ahead of the game, change the culture, and return to full health.

The first step is to take charge of the things in your control. Firm up your processes, train everyone, and create strong standards to follow. That way, when the world spins a different direction, your response will be measured and ready. This is management by planning rather than management by crisis.

How do you change a culture so it's alive again? How do you go from the surgeon performing open-heart surgery to the friendly family doctor dispensing advice and aspirin for minor aches and pains?

Our leadership panel tells *what they do to foster a healthy environment*. Here's what they had to say:

Have clear direction and vision

I once interviewed for a position overseeing a large group of employees. As part of the interview process, I was taken to the workplace. I walked in and very soon had a sense of dread. It was disheveled, the employees looked disinterested, and no one looked me in the eye. *Not one person.*

While I could have thrown myself into the fray and tried to turn the culture around, the negativity seemed institutionalized. Fortunately, in the end, I didn't get the job.

You know you're in a healthy environment when you walk in and within five minutes you understand the goals, the mission, and the culture. Unhealthy environments have no goals, and those involved are usually just putting in time.

"I try to remind our team what we are doing, and why we are doing it," said Larry Hyche. It's really that simple. Some hang signs proclaiming the goals and post progress sheets in visible locations. A good communication strategy will integrate the direction and vision into every piece of communication—from the letterhead, to the billboard, to the paycheck. *Never let your team forget what they are doing and why they are doing it.*

As members of any organization, we want to know that what we do is important, that it matters! Settling for anything less than the best is a disservice to you, those you lead, and your organization. Mediocrity removes the air from the room, leaving us gasping on past success and little hope for the future.

DISPLAY OPEN COMMUNICATIONS, WITH CLARITY

We've discussed communications plenty in this book. And we'll continue to talk about it in every subsequent presentation, demonstration, and discussion—it's just that important. The mere fact we keep repeating the significance of communication is a good example for you and your organization. If you believe in something, you'll talk about it, reinforce it, and then talk about it again. And again.

"We waste people's time when they have to navigate ambiguity every day," said Rebecca Morlando. Her point? "Don't keep them guessing."

There is something to be said about simplicity. When 3M tells their employees that their mission is "Innovation," that sends a message. Verizon's slogan is, "Make Progress Every Day" and that tells a story. Goldman Sachs tells their employees, "Our Client's Interests Always Come First."

Now anyone can hire a wordsmith to find a great couple of words and then hire a graphic designer to design a logo. But to live out that brand takes something entirely different.

Simple. Clear. Real.

Beyond slogans, the daily communications must also foster clarity. How you choose to do that sets the tone for a healthy environment. Open doors, frequent stand ups, question-and-answer sessions—they give a chance for all parties to "clear the air."

Kelly Jackson has both an open door and regular meetings to present information. "This way we communicate what is going on, dispel rumors, perform informal training, and answer questions."

Larry Hyche manages paid church staff as well as volunteers, so he has to communicate in a variety of ways. "I want everyone to have a voice and feel like they are valued."

A healthy organization is one where there is a family atmosphere—and just like in any family, there will be disagreement. I was friends with a full- blooded Italian during college. I would go over to his house, where his mama fussed over me and made sure I was fed. But it was foreign for me to see how passionately they "talked" with each other over issues. With full expression and emotion they "discussed" things. But then they would come to the table, hold hands, and pray. And no one could love like they did.

Is there a proper balance between disagreement and agreement? I think so.

"We have to have openness to discuss issues," said Mike Stanfield. "It's hard, but we strive to provide an environment where concerns can be raised without any fear of reprisals."

There might be some sauce spilled on the floor, but in the end, everyone loves the meal.

GIVE AND RECEIVE FREQUENT FEEDBACK

On the heels of communication is frequent feedback. In my observations over the years, the organizations with the best feedback processes were generally the healthiest. When every person knows their place in the organization and how they are personally and corporately performing, then feedback gives a framework for feedback.

"I intentionally encourage my team and provide feedback so they know they are appreciated—and so they know my expectations," said Kelly Jackson.

Nobody likes to flounder. If you're doing a good job, then you should know it. If you're doing a bad job, then someone should tell you so you can improve or get out of the way.

I had a boss who waited until the year-end review to give any feedback at all. I sat in the dark for a full twelve months wondering how I was doing. Worse, those yearly reviews were full of items he had stuck in his folder—petty mistakes that could have been resolved on the spot rather than months and months later, when memories were dim and a proper time for response had long passed.

Fortunately, I was motivated enough to work for a higher calling and simply performed to my best.

Gary Abney not only doesn't wait, he "coaches forward." "I paint a picture of what appropriate behavior is expected. We then agree on a plan on how to move toward that goal." That kind of attitude provides a great framework for frequent feedback.

TRUST IS PARAMOUNT

"Trust must be earned. It's never simply given," says John Dupes. He's right. Too many leaders think that trust goes along with the title. It doesn't. In fact, the only guarantee is that you'll be *distrusted* at the outset. Everyone will be testing you, to see your mettle, to find out exactly what you are made of. They'll look for you to violate what little trust they place in you.

And it only takes a single act. But if you pass the test, they give you more trust.

Leaders must keep their word. When you say something

or make a commitment, then do what you said you would. If you can't fulfill a promise, then don't hide or cover it up. Be upfront, honest, and open, and by doing so you will gain legions of followers.

"Any team will thrive if they know the leader behind them understands the importance of their respective contribution," adds John.

Paul Bishop facilitates health in his organization by exhibiting grace. This is the concept of allowing others to fail, forgiving quickly, and restoring and making right. "Give others more grace than they expect. This shows an ability to work with others." This respect will foster a returned trust.

WORK HARD, BUT MAKE TIME TO PLAY

A healthy team knows how to pull together to overcome a difficulty. They know how to coalesce to finish a project. And they know how to let their hair down.

"We want to work hard, and then we want to play hard," said Bobby Welch. "We want people to give maximum service and effort during the work day. Then we provide down time where we fellowship and enjoy non-work related activities."

At Bobby's company they have monthly catered lunches, annual fall tail-gate parties, movie nights, and celebrations for accomplishments.

There is a rhythm of work and play that is a natural part of who we are. That's where the term "Sabbath-rest" came from—a chance to reenergize the body, mind, and soul.

Dan Roloff of Foundations for Laity Renewal communicates often on the concept of leisure, play, and relaxation, and how it relates to productive work. "As a people, we don't value play," he writes. "Instead, we talk about work, purpose, and achievement."

He sees play exhibited in one of two ways. One is where we release pent-up emotions through our leisure. We are stressed at work, so we go for a run to blow it off. We have an angry telephone conversation, so we go to the gym.

The other type of play is to sharpen our skills so we feel like we can have an impact on what's happening around us. That's why businessmen play golf and young executives race bikes.

He's an advocate for simply letting leisure sometimes be about nothing. Organizations would be wise to institute time-outs as well—planned periods of rest, play, and interaction with no other goal but enjoyment.

It recharges us, refreshes our minds, and replenishes our spirits. A healthy team is one where time off is honored, vacations are celebrated, and evenings protected. And sometimes, on a sunny Friday, the boss brings everyone to a park for a hamburger, some horseshoes, and laughter.

Come Monday, he'll see the best productivity yet.

SET THE EXAMPLE

A healthy organization has clear roles. There are senior leaders, and depending on the size, middle and first-line leaders. And there are those who follow the leaders. Too many organizations have

> "A healthy team is one where time off is honored, where vacations are celebrated, and evenings protected"

moved to an empowering model that gives *every* person an equal vote, an equal say. This model looks good on paper—just like socialism looks good to some. But in reality, it rarely works.

A better alternative is to narrow the extremes, bringing the top end of leadership closer to the entry level. Nothing ruins a culture of cooperation than the perception that leadership is overly privileged.

"A leader must be willing to get dirty, to get in the trenches," said John Dupes. "But he doesn't stay there, but shows they are not above the task at hand. This demonstrates that every position is important."

Think about the message separate parking spaces, bathrooms, and break rooms send. There is a joy that goes with leadership, and yes, the salary and compensation should be commensurate with the added responsibility. But it's a mistake to create a separate class, a caste system of haves and have-nots.

"Lead by example," advises Kristy Knight. "I do not ask those that I lead to do something I am not willing to do myself."

Just think of those great battle scenes in the movies, like William Wallace in *Braveheart*. Because he was lion-hearted, so were his men.

When the team is asked to stay late, then your light should be on too. When everyone has to take a temporary pay cut, then yours should be the first. When the air conditioning is not functioning, don't sneak a portable unit into your office.

If there are rules on attendance, dress, and personal calls, then they should apply to you. Leadership has its benefits—but they should never be contrary to the limits everyone else abides by.

"Demonstrate your commitment by living the same rules as you expect your employees to," said Ian Poulton.

BE AWARE OF THE CULTURE

The culture of an organization is a tricky thing. That's why some leaders are complete failures in one situation but an absolute success when they move to another.

Though it's tough to change a culture, it can be done. But

it's a slow process, and the foolish leader is the one who tries too much, too fast.

Set the vision, and then work with the culture of the organization to meet it.

"My role is to serve the team's vision and each member of the team in the pursuit of that vision," said Gary Abney.

Self-awareness for organizations is as important as self-awareness for leaders. What is your group known for? What are their traits? What makes them different than competitors or peers? Help your team figure out their identity and then build on it. If they are known for quality, then celebrate that. If they are known for efficient service, then laud them for that.

On the other hand, if they are known for being hostile to newcomers, help them identify that weakness. If they are known for a shoddy product, then recognize it and overcome the shortcoming through training and standards.

DEVELOP A SYSTEM OF REWARD, AFFIRMATION, AND ACCOUNTABILITY

You can foster a healthy environment by rewarding effort, dealing with poor performance, and holding everyone accountable.

"Maintain a fair and just environment," advises Mike Stanfield. "If employees feel unfairly treated or that justice doesn't exit, they will be disillusioned and disenfranchised."

We've previously talked about rewards, but an organization that not only rewards team members but celebrates as a whole is certain to have a positive and healthy atmosphere.

Ian Poulton tells us to invest in the workspace. "Make it inviting. Give them the right tools to get the job done." Then you can begin to work on the deeper things like attitude. Investing in the workspace is affirming, telling others that they mean something and are a worthy investment.

CHALLENGE EACH OTHER TO GROW INDIVIDUALLY

We constantly have to evaluate our organizations. Are we growing? Are we moving in the right direction? And those questions apply to us individually, too. We can ride the dinosaur until it's extinct, or we can build a dynasty that will continue to prosper.

Dynasty makers don't get comfortable and they don't take things for granted. They never forget where they are going and they always remember where they are going.

We have a tendency to stay "safe." Thomas Watson, the one-time chairman of IBM, observed this.

"Safe is for storing valuables. Safe is good for the tires on your car. But in business, I've never been a fan of 'better safe than sorry.'"

> "We can ride the dinosaur until it's extinct, or we can build a dynasty that will continue to prosper."

We have a tendency to get comfortable in our positions, in our knowledge, and in our places. But what sets us apart is the relentless passion to find better ways to perform. Seeking continual improvement will help us compete, survive, and even thrive in the future. Your job is to set the pace—to look, to learn, and to lead.

In other words, get uncomfortable.

FINAL THOUGHTS

THE EDGE

"The winner's edge is not in a gifted birth, a high IQ, or in talent. The winner's edge is all in the attitude, not aptitude. Attitude is the criterion for success." – Dennis Waitley

"The secret of success is constancy of purpose." – Benjamin Disraeli

Do you ever feel like your organization is run by a coin toss? Heads you take one path. Tails you go another. And neither choice is attractive?

On one side we have the past, filled with both success and failure. We bask in the wins and try to forget the losses. We carry the memories of yesterday like a heavy pack. The broken relationships, failed ideas, and perceptions out of control are an option we simply do not want to live with.

On the other side is the future. Tomorrow's thoughts are exciting but are often filled with the fear of the unknown. We either brace for the next big chance or hope to hang on for the ride.

But think of a third option – the edge. We don't need to live in the past or hope for the future, but live in the now. Living on the edge of today will allow you to make the most of your position not by the force of authority, but by the persuasiveness of character.

We hope you'll take the principles of these few pages to heart; that you'll realize that you can grow as a leader, and by doing so, you'll make a difference.

Dr. Larry Little is the principal and CEO of the Enrichment Center Group, an international force in coaching current leaders and shaping the next generation. As an author and executive coach, he speaks to the hearts of organizations and their leaders. His unique approach focuses on building relationships between the values of the organization and its members through thoughtful, intentional leadership. Thousands of modern leaders are now impacting every kind of organization from Fortune 500 companies to football teams. You'll find him on the lecture circuit, in seminars, or in one-on-one coaching sessions with leaders who want to make a difference.

Melissa Hambrick Jackson is a skilled business leader, executive coach, and motivational trailblazer. She serves as the principal business partner and COO of The Enrichment Center Group. In her position, she works with leaders around the world to develop effective strategies for group leadership and individual success. She gets results through emphasizing the power of relationship, the strength of consistency, and the belief in bringing the best out in people. As a skilled speaker and facilitator, she has the ability to connect leaders to those they lead.

David Rupert has written extensively about the relationship between the workplace and the contemporary employee for the past three decades. He's lived those challenges as a line worker, supervisor, and manager in a variety of settings. He's also served as a workplace chaplain, motivational speaker, and a writer and editor for organizational leaders. David has more than 500 articles on leadership to accompany nearly 700 other published articles. He currently serves as an editor at The High Calling. You can find him on a Colorado River or at www.davidrupert.net.

Dr. Larry Little is the principal and CEO of the Enrichment Center Group, an international force in coaching current leaders and shaping the next generation. As an author and executive coach, he speaks to the hearts of organizations and their leaders. His unique approach focuses on building relationships between the values of the organization and its members through thoughtful, intentional leadership. Thousands of modern leaders are now impacting every kind of organization from Fortune 500 companies to football teams. You'll find him on the lecture circuit, in seminars, or in one-on-one coaching sessions with leaders who want to make a difference.

Melissa Hambrick Jackson is a skilled business leader, executive coach, and motivational trailblazer. She serves as the principal business partner and COO of The Enrichment Center Group. In her position, she works with leaders around the world to develop effective strategies for group leadership and individual success. She gets results through emphasizing the power of relationship, the strength of consistency, and the belief in bringing the best out in people. As a skilled speaker and facilitator, she has the ability to connect leaders to those they lead.

David Rupert has written extensively about the relationship between the workplace and the contemporary employee for the past three decades. He's lived those challenges as a line worker, supervisor, and manager in a variety of settings. He's also served as a workplace chaplain, motivational speaker, and a writer and editor for organizational leaders. David has more than 500 articles on leadership to accompany nearly 700 other published articles. He currently serves as an editor at The High Calling. You can find him on a Colorado River or at www.davidrupert.net.